W9-BSC-463

INSIGHT ⊙ GUIDES

EXPLORE

DUBAI

⊙ Walking Eye App

Your guide now includes a free eBook to your chosen destination, for the same great price as before. Simply download the Walking Eye App from the App Store or Google Play to access your free eBook.

HOW THE WALKING EYE APP WORKS

Through the Walking Eye App, you can purchase a range of eBooks and destination content. However, when you buy this book, you can download the corresponding eBook for free. Just see below in the grey panel where to find your free content and then scan the QR code at the bottom of this page.

Destinations: Download essential destination content featuring recommended sights and attractions, restaurants, hotels and an A–Z of practical information, all available for purchase.

Ships: Interested in ship reviews? Find independent reviews of river and ocean ships in this section, all available for purchase.

ebooks: You can download your free accompanying digital version of this guide here. You will also find a whole range of other eBooks, all available for purchase.

Free access to travel-related blog articles about different destinations, updated on a daily basis.

HOW THE EBOOKS WORK

The eBooks are provided in EPUB file format. Please note that you will need an eBook reader installed on your device to open the file. Many devices come with this as standard, but you may still need to install one manually from Google Play.

The eBook content is identical to the content in the printed guide.

HOW TO DOWNLOAD THE WALKING EYE APP

1. Download the Walking Eye App from the App Store or Google Play.
2. Open the app and select the scanning function from the main menu.
3. Scan the QR code on this page – you will then be asked a security question to verify ownership of the book.
4. Once this has been verified, you will see your eBook in the purchased ebook section, where you will be able to download it.

Other destination apps and eBooks are available for purchase separately or are free with the purchase of the Insight Guide book.

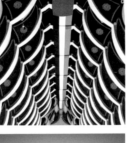

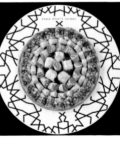

CONTENTS

A DESERT EXPERIENCE

No visit to Dubai is complete without a trip to experience the stark, serene beauty of the desert (route 8), or to tear it up dune bashing or quad biking on the towering dunes.

RECOMMENDED ROUTES FOR...

DUBAI FROM THE WATER

Abras are a common Dubai transport and a delightful way for visitors to take in views of the dramatic skyline along the Creek (route 1); for an alternative watery experience take a trip on a sightseeing dhow (route 7).

HEDONISTIC HOTELS

Dubai has some of the biggest, glitziest and the most downright stunning hotels on the planet, enscapsulated by the iconic, 'seven-star' Burj Al Arab (route 5).

HIT THE BEACHES

Dubai's coastline has numerous classy beach resorts (route 5 and route 6) but for some of the more off-the-beaten track beaches head to the Northern Emirates or the East Coast (route 10 and route 12).

MODERN ARCHITECTURE

In the last 20 years, Dubai has altered beyond recognition, and it now has a truly 21st-century skyline, best appreciated from Sheikh Zayed Road and Dubai Marina (route 4 and route 6).

OFF THE BEATEN TRACK

A tour round the other emirates gives a flavour of Dubai before the oil boom (route 12 and route 13) and, of course, there are some lovely deserted beaches to discover here too (route 13).

SHOPPING IN SOUKS

For a local shopping experience, try shopping in the traditional souks of Deira (route 2), with cut-price gold, exotic perfumes and spices, and tubs full of fragrant frankincense.

TRADITIONAL DUBAI

Explore the souks, mosques and heritage houses of the old city centre during walking tours of Bur Dubai and Deira (route 1 and route 2).

INTRODUCTION

An introduction to Dubai's geography, customs and culture, plus illuminating background information on cuisine, history and what to do when you're there.

Dubai Marina by night

EXPLORE DUBAI

Dubai is a modern Arabian metropolis, a regional hub for business and leisure and an international crossroads. Visiting this futuristic desert city is a unique and fascinating experience.

Dubai's rise from unknown to household name confirms the adage that in the world of celebrity it can take 20 years to become an overnight success. In the late 1980s, few people outside the oil industry would have found this former fishing and pearling village on a map. In the space of a few decades, the city has transformed itself from a modest Arabian trading town, which few outside the region had ever heard of, into one of the planet's most glamorous, futuristic and talked-about destinations, home to the world's tallest building, its biggest shopping mall, its largest man-made island and a host of other record-busting developments – all of which continue to attract hyperbole, admiration and derision in equal measure.

Dubai has now become a byword for a certain type of high-octane glamour and a major celebrity destination, with, among others, film star George Clooney making his movie *Syriana* here, Morgan Freeman being a regular at its annual film festival, and cricketer Andrew Flintoff now a regular with a home on the luxurious Palm Jumeirah, while countless others are regularly spotted, from sports stars and their WAGs to major film and music stars living the high life and enjoying a bit of the emirate's near year-round sunshine.

The city suffered particularly badly during the credit crunch of 2008–09, with numerous articles in the international press chronicling Dubai's alleged demise, complete with the disastrous collapse of its real-estate market and incipient bankruptcy (staved off thanks to a last-minute cash injection from neighbouring Abu Dhabi). After some lean years and reigning in of its wildest ambition and projects, the city is once again beginning to recapture its famed commercial verve and vibrancy, and with the announcement of Dubai as the host for Expo 2020, development is picking up and the outlook is positive.

Dubai continues to divide opinion. Politically stable, commercially dynamic and tolerant of other cultures and religions, for some, it's one of the 21st-century's great urban experiments; an attempt to create a truly global city at the heart of one of the world's most turbulent regions.

URBAN AREAS

Dubai is the second city (after Abu Dhabi) of the United Arab Emirates

A 4x4 safari in the desert

(UAE), a federation of seven sheikh-doms on the Arabian (Persian) Gulf. The city is bounded by the sea to the west, the emirates of Sharjah and Abu Dhabi to the north and south, and by desert to the east. The city's inhospitable environment has not curtailed its ambition, and huge land-reclamation projects, oil wealth, bulldozers and seawater-desalination plants have all played a part in taming the desert.

City hubs

Dubai is a linear city, stretching from north to south down the coast of the UAE for well over 20km (12 miles). The original centre of the metropolis can be found along the Creek, at the northern end of the city, flanked by the communities of Shindagha, Bur Dubai and Deira. The modern city has since expanded gradually southwards from here, spreading down the Jumeira coast and the parallel Sheikh Zayed Road before reaching the huge new Downtown Dubai development, roughly at the midpoint of the modern city. South of here development continues, eventually reaching the huge new Dubai Marina.

Transport within the city has been revolutionised over the past few years following the opening of the Dubai Metro, which provides a convenient way of making trips across the city that would previously have required a car, and the first tram line in 2014. New Metro lines and planned extensions should further improve matters. For now, however, most residents continue to get around by car, and traffic jams are an established fact of city life.

THE DESERT

Dubai is the capital of the emirate of Dubai, which covers some 3,900 sq km (1,506 miles). While the city itself is flat, the topography inland consists of rolling dunes and the foothills of the Hajar Mountains. Climbing to a peak of 2,000m (6,560ft), the Hajar range separates Dubai from the Arabian Gulf – just over an hour's drive from the city. The desert is a playground for residents with four-wheel drive vehicles, motorbikes and quad bikes; for visitors, an off-road desert safari with a local tour operator is a must. The UAE's largest desert conservation reserve centres around the luxury Al Maha Desert Resort, where rare Arabian oryx roam free.

CLIMATE

Summers in Dubai are very hot and humid. From May to September daytime temperatures rarely fall below 40°C (104°F), with humidity up to 90 per cent. From October to April, the weather resembles an extremely good European summer, with temperatures hovering around 30°C (mid-80s°F) and with little or no humidity. Evenings can feel chilly in January and February, when sweaters may be required.

Emirati dress at World Art Dubai

Rainfall

Annual rainfall is minimal (an average of 42mm/1.5in), but downpours can occur between November and March; when it rains, it pours, so if you plan to explore a *wadi* (dry river bed), check that it is not raining in the mountains, otherwise you could be caught in a flood. Inland, Hatta is a cool retreat from the more humid coast.

Parks and reserves

For such a built-up city, Dubai is surprisingly well provided with parks. Most are open from 8am until well after dark; most charge small entrance fees. Perhaps the best park within the city limits is the expansive Creekside Park (see page 43). Other green spaces include Safa Park (see page 57, Sun–Wed 8am–10pm, Thu–Sat 8am–11pm), between southern Jumeira and Sheikh Zayed Road, a favourite with joggers and local youngsters drawn by its fairground attractions. The attractive Al Mamzar Beach Park (see page 23) is another favourite thanks to its fine stretches of beach and expansive parkland areas.

The low-key Ras Al Khor Wildlife Sanctuary is an important stopover on winter migratory routes from East Africa to West Asia for almost 70 species of birds, and is best known for its flocks of bright pink flamingos – one of Dubai's most surreal sights.

WHEN TO GO

November to April is when the climate is at its best. It is then that Dubai's lively sports and social scenes come to life. However, before you book, it is advisable to check when the holy month of Ramadan falls, as there will be restrictions on music and nightlife.

Visiting during the scorching summer months is less appealing, and your holiday may be based around water and indoor activities, although on the plus side, rates at many of the city's upmarket hotels and resorts can fall dramatically.

POPULATION

Dubai's population had reached almost 2.5 million in 2015, while the population of the UAE as a whole is one of the fastest-growing in the Arab world, hovering close to the 9 million mark. Dubai is also one of the world's most multicultural cities. Over 90 per cent of residents are expatriates, ranging from low-wage Indian and Pakistani construction workers and Filipino waitresses through to more affluent expat Arabs from the Levant and North Africa, as well as a sizeable community of European and North American professionals. Emiratis in Dubai thus find themselves in the curious position of being virtual foreigners in their own city, and it's possible to visit Dubai and meet very few Emirati nationals except for those at airport immigration and the tourist information counters in malls.

Sheikh Zayed Grand Mosque

Jumeirah Dar Al Masyaf

DON'T LEAVE DUBAI WITHOUT...

Exploring Downtown Dubai. The new centre of Dubai is home to the world's tallest building, Burj Khalifa (take a tour to the top), the world's largest water fountain display and the biggest shopping mall, The Dubai Mall. See page 48.

Dune dinner. See the best of the desert with an exciting 4WD drive over the dunes, ending up at an Arabic campsite for a camel ride at sunset, a meal under the stars, and traditional dancing. See page 71.

An evening at Madinat. Head there in the late afternoon for a view in the daylight, enjoy a happy hour cocktail at Bahri Bar watching the sunset, then explore the souk and dine at one of the waterfront restaurants. See page 59.

Shop in the souks. Head to Deira for the Gold Souk and the Spice Souk, or Bur Dubai's 'Old Souk' (Textile Souk), for bustling traditional markets packed with atmosphere and character. See pages 29 and 38.

Hit the beach. Enjoy a day at The Beach in Dubai Marina with a beautiful sandy beach, gorgeous sea, plenty to do on and at The Walk, and spectacular views. See page 61.

Shopping malls. Dubai's malls offer an incredible variety of options for shopping, leisure and dining – especially useful in the hotter months. See page 51.

Enjoy an Arabian feast. Settle yourself in for an evening at one of Dubai's plentiful Arabic restaurants and order a full selection of mezze, grills and *manakish*, all accompanied by amazing fruit juices. See page 16.

Cross the creek by abra. At Dhs1, this is one of the cheapest activities in Dubai, and one of the most memorable: with an *abra* ride between Bur Dubai and Deira offering a very local experience, as well as fantastic views. See page 30.

Step back in time. Areas such as the Al Fahidi Historical Neighbourhood, Bur Dubai and Shindagha are home to some of Dubai's most historic buildings, giving a flavour of what life was like in the Emirates in days gone by. See page 28.

Visit a mosque. A rare chance to see inside a mosque when visiting the vast and impressive Sheikh Zayed Grand Mosque in Abu Dhabi or the smaller, but beautiful Jumeira Mosque in Dubai offers an informative insight into Islamic religion and culture. See pages 55 and 93.

The east coast tour. A day trip to the east of the UAE takes you through the desert and mountains, past historical and heritage sites, alongside open beaches with the crystal waters of the Gulf of Oman, ideal for diving and snorkelling. See page 86.

The garden city. Located across the desert from Dubai, the city of Al Ain is a great destination for a day out, with vast oases to stroll through, forts and heritage sites to explore, and the best zoo and safari park in the UAE. See page 83.

The Bedu

One of the oldest tribespeople in the world, the Bedu (Bedouin) were once nomadic herdsmen, living off the products of their animals. Today, however, Bedu culture and lifestyle are under threat from the modernisation that oil wealth has brought to the Emirates.

National Dress

UAE national dress is worn in the workplace, at home and when out and about. The men's white, floor-length robe is known as the *kandoora* or *dishdasha*. The cloth headdress, which can be white or red-and-white check, is a *gutra*, secured by a stiff black cord known as an *agal*, with which their Bedu ancestors hobbled their camels' legs – although among young men baseball caps are increasingly replacing the *gutra* and *agal*.

The most visible items of women's clothing are the floor-length black cloak, the *abaya*, and headscarf, called a *sheyla*. Older women may be seen wearing the stiff gold and lacquer facemask known as a *burqa*, though this is becoming less common. Children often dress in Western-style clothes.

Given the number of different nationalities resident in Dubai – upwards of 180 – you are actually more likely to hear Hindi, Urdu, Malayalam and Tagalog than Arabic. While Arabic is the UAE's official language, English is widely spoken and used for everyday contact between the various groups.

EXPERIENCING BOTH SIDES OF DUBAI

Dubai can offer budget travellers a surprising amount to see and do, but this is definitely a place to let your hair down and if your budget is reasonably flexible, it's one of the world's best places to indulge in luxury living. Here you can dress up and go all out: treat yourself to sundowner cocktails in fabulous bars overlooking the sea; dine at some of the world's best restaurants owned by international celebrity chefs; enjoy afternoon tea in hip hotels with views to die for; experience beach parties with vibes like a Middle Eastern version of Ibiza; and seek out the most glamorous nightclubs.

On the other hand, as well as the glitz and glamour (along with the fairytale Arabian-palace themed hotels), Dubai is a city with a very real heart where life goes on just as it has for decades, if not hundreds of years. This side of the city, including the areas around the creek with the traditional souks, the heritage areas and historical sites; bustling streets with hundreds of cheap shops and restaurants to discover; and everyday folk commuting across the creek by *abra*, gives visitors a flavour of the real emirates from before the oil-money and international ambition changed it, and it is still going to remain here, as much as some parts of the city change.

Dubai's futuristic skyline

TOP TIPS FOR VISITING DUBAI

Zero tolerance. Dubai has a zero-tolerance approach to drink driving. The penalty for being found with the smallest amount of alcohol in your blood can be a month in jail, with more severe penalties for causing death through drink driving. The bottom line is that if you're going to drink alcohol, take a taxi.

Ramadan rules. Whatever your religion, it is illegal to eat in public in daylight during the holy month of Ramadan, when Muslims abstain from food and drink (and smoking) from sunrise to sunset. Some restaurants open for lunch but screen off their eating areas. Although pork and alcohol are not consumed by Muslims, several hotel restaurants use them as ingredients in certain dishes. These will be highlighted with a symbol on the menu.

Dress appropriately. In addition to dressing appropriately, before entering Jumeirah Mosque or Sheikh Zayed Grand Mosque, you will be required to remove your shoes and enter in bare feet, as is the custom. You should also be sure to remove your shoes at the Cultural Centre.

Souk opening hours. There are no official opening hours in Bur Dubai and Deira's souks, although most shops usually open Sat–Thu 10am–1pm and 4–10pm, Fri 4–10pm; some shops in more touristy areas might also stay open throughout the afternoon.

Shopping habits. Don't assume that because of Dubai's tax-free reputation, everything here is cheaper than elsewhere in the world. You can bargain for deals in the souks, but not in malls, except perhaps when buying carpets or large souvenirs, and you are more likely to get a large discount with cash.

Bargaining. If you are interested in buying something in the souks, don't reveal your full interest to the seller. Start your offer low – at around half the amount you estimate you would finally like to spend.

Duty free. You can actually buy duty free when arriving at Dubai's airport, and with some really cheap prices (compared to hotel bars), you might be glad to have it with you (alcohol can't be consumed in public or out of licensed premises such as hotels).

Get lost. Make the effort to explore off the beaten track, wandering around in Bur Dubai, Deira or even Sharjah, where there are sights, sounds and places to discover around every corner.

Get out of town. While Dubai has more than enough to keep you entertained for your holiday, venturing out into the real UAE will surprise you with the vast range of landscapes across the country: from snorkelling among the coral and multi-coloured marine life around Snoopy Island on the East Coast to relaxing on top of a sand dune after an afternoon of desert driving, or even strolling round the forts and oases in Al Ain.

Seafood at Pierchic

FOOD AND DRINK

From simple Emirati dishes with lamb or fish to colourful Moroccan feasts, Dubai offers visitors the Arab world on a plate. But this cosmopolitan city is also a culinary melting pot that caters for diverse international tastes.

Dubai's local eating out guides bulge with details of an expanding number of restaurants serving authentic cuisine from all over the world. From alfresco Lebanese eateries to hip New Zealand-owned cafés and no-frills sushi bars, Dubai offers rich pickings for tastebud tourists. It may be a Muslim society, but visitors will find a liberal attitude to the sale of pork and alcohol.

Note that Dubai tends to dine late at night, so for a good atmosphere plan dinner from around 9pm. If you're heading for a hotel venue, book in advance. Major credit and debit cards are widely accepted, although smaller, cheaper places may only accept cash.

WORLD-CLASS CUISINE

For dedicated diners, whether carnivorous or vegetarian, Dubai has all the ingredients for memorable meals, from delicious street food right up to fine dining in luxury hotels. Given the increasingly cosmopolitan nature of both its inhabitants and visitors, it is little surprise that Dubai has developed into a regional centre for world-class cuisine.

Many of Dubai's finest restaurants are located in hotels and sports clubs that are vibrant social centres for nationals, expatriates and visitors alike. Venues that have a number of different food outlets and bars feel like mini-neighbourhoods. And in contrast to the majority of 'high street' and mall restaurants, all hotels are licensed to sell alcohol.

For a combination of excellent food and pitch-perfect ambience, consider the seafood restaurants Al Mahara at Burj Al Arab and Pierchic at Al Qasr, Zheng He's Chinese at Mina A'Salam and Italian restaurant Alta Badia for the views high up in Emirates Towers. For Arabic food, try the Lebanese restaurant Al Qasr Dubai Marine Beach Resort or Emirates Towers' Al Nafoorah.

Outside the hotels

Away from hotels, more 'real' dining experiences can be found all over town, including Arabic food in popular chains such as Beirut, Automatic and Zaatar W Zeit, as well as independents such as Al Mallah and Khan Murjan, which offer excellent value for money. Popular cafes include the funky Dutch-owned More café near Dubai Mall and the Lime Tree Café on

Arabic cusine at Al Iwan

Indian street food at the Textile Souk

Jumeira Road. Areas such as Karama and Satwa have masses of options for cheap eats such as Pakistani, Indian, Filipino and Sri Lankan, including standout restaurants such as Ravis for cheap, spicy curries, and Saravanna Bhavan for amazingly priced South Indian food including *dosa* and *thali* set meals.

If you need fuelling after hours of sightseeing or shopping, every mall has at least one food court, often with some decent stand alone restaurants as well.

ARABIC CUISINE

In the main, for Arabic food read Lebanese. Mezze – small dishes and dips – are the Middle East's equivalent of tapas. Staple mezze to scoop up with flat Arabic bread are: *hummus* (a chickpea dip with olive oil, garlic and lemon juice); *tabbouleh* (finely chopped parsley and mint with tomato and bulgar wheat); *fattoush* (a salad of lettuce, tomato, cucumber with toasted Arabic bread); *moutabel* (similar to hummus, but made with roasted eggplant); and *falafel* (deep-fried, mashed chickpea patties). Mezze are usually followed by a main course such as *shawarma* or grilled meat, but can be a satisfying and filling meal in themselves.

Regional dishes
As with all things Emirati in Dubai, finding somewhere serving the food is quite rare. It is derived from Bedu fare and consists mainly of fish, chicken and lamb served as kebabs or biriani-style with rice. *Mach-*

boos is spiced lamb with rice, *harees* is slow-cooked wheat and lamb, and *fareed* is a meat and vegetable stew poured over thin bread. Arabic desserts typically feature nuts, syrup and cream. Popular puddings include *Umm Ali* ('Mother of Ali'), a bread and butter pudding with sultanas and coconut, topped with nuts; and *Kashta*, clotted cream topped with pistachio, pine seeds and honey.

DRINKS

As most Arabic restaurants don't serve alcohol, try one of the tasty fresh mixed fruit juices such as 'fruit cocktail' or the outstanding lemon and mint. Traditional Arabian coffee (*kahwa*) is flavoured with cardamom and served in small, handleless cups. Thick Turkish coffee is more commonly served in restaurants. If you don't like your coffee sweet, ask for 'medium sweet' or 'without sugar'. Arabic-style tea, also served sweet, is without milk, flavoured with cardamom or mint.

Food and drink prices

Throughout this book, this is the price guide for a two-course meal for two, with a glass of wine each where alcohol is available:

$$$$$ = over Dhs500
$$$$ = Dhs400–500
$$$ = Dhs200–400
$$ = Dhs100–200
$ = below Dhs100

Wandering the Textile Souk

SHOPPING

For many visitors, Dubai's various attractions – from the cultural to the rest-and-recreation variety – are mere sideshows to the main event: its shops. For dedicated shoppers, Dubai is the proverbial paradise.

Shopping in Dubai takes two forms. The first is in the old-fashioned souks (markets) of Deira and Bur Dubai, where you'll find traditional Arabian produce, artefacts, gold, spices, perfumes, material and clothes, lined up for sale in myriad shoe-box shops. Prices are generally cheap, although bargaining is essential. The second is in the city's vast array of modern malls, which offer popular brands, designer fashions, fabulously expensive watches and jewelleryaplenty, alongside souvenirs and items with a local flavour – while the eye-popping designs and attractions of some malls makes them virtually tourist attractions in their own right.

Dubai Shopping Festival

The annual Dubai Shopping Festival (www.visitdubai.com) takes place every January, and while there are deals, promotions and some discounts available, the whole city has even more of a buzz about it during this month, with shows, events, special attractions and fireworks every night. Check the website for full details.

SOUKS

For bargains and a vibrant atmosphere, nothing beats a visit to the traditional souks.

The most famous is Deira's Gold Souk, one of the cheapest places in the world to buy the precious metal, while the nearby Spice and Perfume souks in Deira Old Souk stock a wide range of spices and scents.

Across the Creek in Bur Dubai, the Textile Souk is the place to head for cheap fabrics and cheesy souvenirs. Karama Shopping Complex is another place for not necessarily genuine bargains.

Also worth exploring are the city's modern 'souks' – replica bazaars built in faux-Arabian style, often with spectacular décor (and air-conditioned comfort) – Souk Madinat Jumeirah, Khan Murjan and Souk Al Bahar are the best. The best time to shop at the old souks is in the morning and late afternoon to evening; they are often closed over lunch and in the early afternoon, and on Friday mornings. Modern souks follow shopping mall hours.

At a fabric shop in Satwa

All that glitters at the Gold Souk

MALLS

For air-conditioned comfort, convenient access and, in several cases, the wow factor, try Dubai's malls. Most open 10am–10pm, and later during the holidays and Ramadan.

The biggest mall in the city is the mighty Dubai Mall, one of the world's largest, while the huge Mall of the Emirates, near Interchange 4 on Sheikh Zayed Road, is another top shopping destination, home to many upmarket stores, a large Arabian Treasures section for souvenirs and carpets, and Ski Dubai, with surreal views over the indoor ski slopes covered in artificial snow.

The more modest Deira City Centre is a perennial favourite, but vying with Mall of the Emirates as Dubai's swankiest shopping destination are the stately BurJuman Centre, home to Saks Fifth Avenue; and the Egyptian-themed Wafi Mall, both on the Bur Dubai side of the Creek. The zany Ibn Battuta Mall, south of the city, is also worth a visit for its outlandish décor, as is the chintzy Italian-style Mercato Mall in Jumeira.

ON THE STREET

Dubai has very few open-air 'high streets'. Deira's Al Riqqa Road is a pleasant avenue of boutiques, while the parallel Maktoum Road's boutiques include Gianni Versace, Dolce & Gabbana and Cartier. In Satwa, there are small boutiques dotted along 2nd December Street.

Textiles and crafts

If you want colourful silks or textiles, check out the many small shops and tailors in the Textile Souk and along Al Fahidi Street in Bur Dubai, while cheap clothes shops can be found in Karama.

For local artwork, visit the small galleries that have sprung up in and around the Al Fahidi Historical Neighbourhood; in The Gate building on Sheikh Zayed Road; and in Al Quoz arts area. The Market at The Beach, is also a popular 'street market' in Dubai Marina.

Global Village

Situated in the outskirts of Dubai, Global Village is a permanent festival site open every evening through the winter. As well as rides and entertainment, hundreds of international pavilions offer stalls selling traditional items, as well as food from many countries around the world.

Out of town

Neighbouring city Sharjah's Central Souk is an attractive and interesting place to shop, and one of the best places to buy carpets from Iran and Pakistan and 'antiques' such as *khanjars*, the short, curved decorative daggers. If you are travelling out of town, the Friday Market near Masafi on the way to the East Coast, and the roadside stalls selling carpets and pottery on the Hatta road are both worth stopping by. In Al Ain, the Camel Souk is a lively place to watch the buying and selling of camels and other animals.

Dubai World Cup at the Meydan Racecourse

SPORT

Dubai has gained an international reputation for world-class sporting events, and visitors can watch the stars of golf, tennis, rugby, horse racing and other major sports here at various times of the year.

Dubai has a surprisingly extensive range of top-class sporting events, including the world's richest horse race; leading golf, tennis and rugby tournaments and international cricket fixtures; while Abu Dhabi hosts the season-ending Formula 1 Grand Prix. Tickets for all events are surprisingly affordable and fairly easy to get (by European and North American standards), though all events are extremely popular, and it's a good idea to reserve tickets as far in advance as possible.

HORSE RACING

The spectacular new Meydan Racecourse is the prime venue for horse racing in the UAE – a state-of-the-art venue including a strikingly modern stadium, with room for 60,000 spectators, and a 2.4km (1.5 miles) turf track.

The racing season is held during the cooler winter months from November to March, culminating in the prestigious Dubai World Cup (www.dubaiworldcup. com), the world's richest horse race with prize money of $10 million. Race-meets are also a major feature on the city's social calendar, attracting a lively crowd of Emiratis and expats, although no betting is allowed.

GOLF

Dubai has a superb selection of golf courses, which include The Address Montgomerie Dubai golf course (www. themontgomerie.com), the Emirates Golf Club (www.dubaigolf.com/emirates-golf-club.aspx), the Al Badia Golf Club at Dubai Festival City (www.albadiagolfclub. ae), the Arabian Ranches (www.arabian ranchesgolfdubai.com), the Els Club in Dubai Sports City (www.elsclubdubai. com), Dubai Creek Golf & Yacht Club (www.dubaigolf.com/dubai-creek-golf-yacht-club.aspx) and two Greg Norman courses at Jumeirah Golf Estates (www. jumeirahgolfestates.com). The Emirates Golf Club is home to the men's Dubai Desert Classic, part of the European Tour, held annually in November and attracting an elite international field – past winners have included Ernie Els, Colin Montgomerie, Rory McIlroy and Tiger Woods. The Dubai Ladies Masters is also held here. The Earth Course hosts the DP World Tour Championship event on the European Tour.

Powerboat at the Grand Prix

Camels at the Al Marmoum Race Track

TENNIS

The Dubai Tennis Championship (late Feb/early March; www.dubaitennis championships.com) is an established fixture on the men's and women's singles circuit – past winners have included Venus Williams, Justine Henin, Caroline Wozniacki, Andy Roddick, Rafael Nadal, Novak Djokovic, who has won four tournaments, and Roger Federer, who has won the men's event seven times.

RUGBY

The Dubai Rugby Sevens (www.dubai rugby7s.com) is part of the International Rugby Board (IRB) Sevens World Series. The three-day tournament at The Sevens Stadium on the edge of the city on the road to Al Ain is contested by the world's best teams every December – and is accompanied by some of the city's most riotous partying.

CARS, BIKES AND BOATS

The leading regional motorsports event is the season-ending Formula 1 Etihad Airways Abu Dhabi Grand Prix (www. formula1.com/en/championship/ races/2016/Abu_Dhabi), held at Yas Island in mid-November. The Abu Dhabi Desert Challenge (www.abudhabidesert challenge.com), a FIA-sanctioned car and motorbike rally, also takes place in November in the deserts around Abu Dhabi. On road, the racetrack at Dubai Autodrome in Dubailand (www.dubai autodrome.com) hosts various other international events through the year. On the water, the Grand Prix of Dubai – a round of the UIM F1H2O World Offshore powerboat championships (www.f1h2o. com) – takes place off Le Meridien Mina Seyahi, with the local favourites, the Dubai-based Victory team, often right up there in the results.

CRICKET

The 25,000-seater cricket stadium at Dubai Sports City (www.dubaisports city.ae) in Dubailand hosts occasional one-day and Twenty20 internationals between leading teams – England, Australia, New Zealand and Pakistan have all played here in past years.

CAMEL RACING

The traditional local pastime of camel racing is enduringly popular in Dubai, with meets now organised by the Dubai Camel Racing Club (050 658 8528) at the Al Marmoum Race Track on the road to Al Ain some 40km from Dubai off exit 37 for Al Lisaili. Races are held during the cooler winter months from September to May; most start early in the morning (around 6am), and jockeys have been replaced with by small robots controlled by the camels' owners. Call the racetrack for details of events on (050 658 8528), or get some help with the Arabic-only website www.dcrc.ae.

Atlantis Hotel's beach

BEACHES

Dubai's beaches are clean, safe and seldom overcrowded. With the exception of Al Mamzar Beach Park, most are located in the south of the city, while further stretches of sand are appearing around Palm Jumeirah as land–reclamation progresses.

Dubai's Arabian Gulf coastline, with its palm-fringed golden sands and azure waters, is one of the city's major draws. The coastline is straight and flat (if you want a mountain backdrop for your swim, head for the UAE's more rugged east coast on the Gulf of Oman); but the beaches are safe, smooth and sandy, with warm, shallow water. The length of the natural coastline is 72km (45 miles), but land reclamation is extending it by an incredible 1,500km (932 miles), which is longer than the natural coastline of the entire UAE.

The best beaches have been carefully manicured, with trees, lawns or breakwaters added to enhance their appeal, and are swept by tractors first thing in the morning. They certainly deliver the rest and relaxation promised in tourist brochures and holidaymaker's most basic requirements: sun, sand and sea.

KEY POINTS

Before you head to the beach, there are just a few important things to note. There's sometimes a strong undertow and currents in some places along the coast, even in the shallows, and drown-

ings are not unheard of, so be careful. Always swim within sight of a lifeguard and never when the red flag is flying. In terms of cultural considerations, restrictions are minimal – normal beachwear is acceptable, but topless bathing for women is a strict no-no, and no-one should walk around in bathing costumes away from the beach. Other considerations include special days for women and young children only at some beach parks, and, during Ramadan, changes in some beaches' opening times and the absence of refreshments (no adults, even non-Muslims, are allowed to eat or drink in public from sunrise to sunset).

PRIVATE BEACHES

In case your hotel doesn't, most of Dubai's beach hotels offer non-guests the use of the beach, pool and facilities for the day, albeit at often pricey rates (from between Dhs 140 up to Dhs450 per adult for entry, although the higher priced options sometimes include a food allowance). At Jumeirah Beach Hotel, rates are Dhs 300/200 for adults/kids (mid-week), but they include entry to the Wild Wadi Water Park, which isn't far from the ticket price alone,

Lifeguard at the Burj Al Arab hotel

so this is a great deal for a full day in the water and on the beach.

For beaches in Jumeira with more seclusion, facilities, attractive surroundings and greenery than the public beaches, both Dubai Marine Beach Resort & Spa and Nikki Beach Dubai, offer day entry to use the beach, pool and facilities.

PUBLIC BEACHES

A much cheaper alternative is to visit one of Dubai's public beaches, which, with their mix of nationalities and wide range of income groups, are far more representative of the city. On weekends and public holidays these beaches and beach parks become focal points for popular events such as family barbecues and kite-flying festivals.

The best public beach park in the city was Jumeirah Beach Park, but this was closed at the time of writing due to the extension of the Dubai Canal from Business Bay out to the sea. Plans for the mouth of the canal include a new park that may be open for 2017, so check if you're in Dubai after this.

Free beaches (open 24hr) include Jumeira Public Beach, also known as 'Russian Beach' or Jumeira Open Beach; Kite Beach; and 'Sunset Beach', right next to the Burj Al Arab. The strip of public beach at JBR in Dubai Marina, called The Beach, is another attractive option, with loads of smooth sand backdropped by the futuristic high-rise Marina skyline.

In the north of the city, in Deira close to the border with Sharjah, Al Mamzar Beach Park (www.dm.gov.ae; daily 8am–10pm, Thu–Sat 8–1pm, Mon/Wed ladies and children only; Dhs5), has a string of decent beaches, sandy coves, swimming pools and beach cabins (extra charges) in extensive parkland, plus fine views of Sharjah over the lagoon.

WATER PARKS

Dubai's superb, state-of-the-art water parks offer a great way to cool off, and provide maximum thrills for kids and adults alike. Wild Wadi Water Park, next to the Jumeirah Beach Hotel, and Aquaventure at Atlantis on Palm Jumeirah both boast watery thrills and spills, ranging from lazy rivers and wave pools for younger kids through to water slides and power jets. North of Dubai in Umm Al Quwain, Dreamland Aqua Park is an older style park, not as large or flashy as Dubai's, but very large and has loads to do. For a very unusual experience, Al Ain's Wadi Adventure offers swimming, surfing a man-made wave, or even whitewater kayaking, with views of the dry, rocky landscape of Jebel Hafeet, the UAE's second highest mountain.

Midnight dips
If you go for a midnight dip you may see the luminescence of microscopic sea creatures around you – they give off a blue-green light when the water is disturbed.

Sheikh Zayed Bin Sultan al-Nahayan, 1966

HISTORY: KEY DATES

An introduction to the region, from fishing village to economic powerhouse, via the dawn of Islam, the arrival of European powers and the rise of the Maktoum dynasty.

PRE-ISLAM

c.5000 BC	Stone Age settlements are established on the Arabian Gulf coast and in the Hajar Mountains.
2700–2000 BC	A Bronze Age settlement is established at Al Sufouh, Dubai.
1st century BC	An Iron Age village is established at Al Qusais, Dubai.
4th century AD	Christianity arrives in Bet Mazunaye, an area corresponding to the modern UAE and northern Oman.
6th century	The Sassanids establish a trading post in Jumeira. Aramaic is the region's lingua franca.
c.632–5	The Battle of Dibba marks the dawn of the Islamic era on the Arabian peninsula. Arabic replaces Aramaic.

EMERGENCE OF DUBAI

1580	The earliest surviving written reference to 'Dibei' is made by Venetian jeweller Gasparo Balbi.
1793	Dubai, a fishing and pearling village of 1,200 people, is a dependency of Abu Dhabi.
1822	A British treaty with Mohammed Bin Hazza is the first recognition on paper that Dubai is a separate entity to more powerful Abu Dhabi and Sharjah.
1833	Maktoum Bin Buti Al Maktoum and 800 members of the Bani Yas tribe arrive in Shindagha from Abu Dhabi. The rule of the Maktoum family begins.
1894	Sheikh Maktoum Bin Hasher uses tax concessions to encourage foreign merchants to settle in Dubai.
1929	Wall Street crash causes pearl prices to fall. The subsequent introduction of the Japanese cultured pearl sounds the industry's death knell and plunges Dubai into an economic depression.

Dubai celebrates the opening of Palm Jumeirah in 2008

POST WORLD WAR II

1958	Sheikh Rashid Bin Saeed Al Maktoum, the 'father of modern Dubai', becomes ruler.
1966	Oil is discovered in Dubai. Exports begin within three years.
1971	The United Arab Emirates (UAE) is established with Abu Dhabi ruler Sheikh Zayed Bin Sultan Al Nahyan as President and Dubai's Sheikh Rashid as Vice President.
1985	Dubai-based airline Emirates is established.

MODERN ERA

1990	Sheikh Rashid dies. He is succeeded by his son Sheikh Maktoum Bin Rashid Al Maktoum.
1994	Sheikh Maktoum's brother, Sheikh Mohammed Bin Rashid Al Maktoum, is made Crown Prince of Dubai.
1996	The Dubai Strategic Plan indicates that oil will run out by 2010; plans are made to diversify the economy.
2001	Following a boom in tourism, work begins on Palm Jumeirah and Palm Jebel Ali, two man-made, palm-shaped islands.
2002	The government announces 100 percent freehold ownership for non-nationals, unleashing a construction boom.
2004	Sheikh Zayed, the founder and President of the UAE, dies at the age of 86. His son Sheikh Khalifa becomes President.
2006	Sheikh Maktoum dies aged 62. His brother Sheikh Mohammed succeeds him as Ruler of Dubai and Prime Minister of the UAE.
2008	The credit crunch hits Dubai, pushing the emirate to the brink of bankruptcy and stalling many major construction projects.
2010	Opening of the Burj Khalifa.
2013	Dubai is announced as the venue for World Expo 2020.
2015	Design set for the Expo Burj 2020 District. A fire on New Year's Eve at The Address Downtown Dubai, previously the seventh tallest hotel in the world, destroys the building.
2016	Emaar announce yet another tower, even taller than the Burj Khalifa, to be ready for 2020.
2017	Mohammed bin Rashid Al Maktoum Solar Park to come online, helping to make to 7 percent of all Dubai's energy to be supplied by renewable sources by 2020.

BEST ROUTES

Al Fahidi Fort at night

BUR DUBAI

This leisurely walking route begins with a visit to the excellent Dubai Museum, followed by a stroll through Bur Dubai's Old Souk and the fine old traditional districts of the Al Fahidi Historical Neighbourhood and Shindagha, before continuing down the waterside to admire the modern buildings lining the Creek.

> **DISTANCE:** 4.5km (3 miles)
> **TIME:** A full day
> **START:** Dubai Museum, Bur Dubai
> **END:** Al Seef Abra Station, Bur Dubai
> **POINTS TO NOTE:** Take a taxi to the starting point of this walking tour.

Dubai has developed spectacularly in the past 50 years. What was once a small fishing and trading community has become a commercial and leisure hub with towering concrete, metal-and-glass structures. Separating Bur Dubai from Deira, and cutting through the historic heart of a now sprawling metropolis, the Creek is much changed from the 1940s when British flying boats touched down here en route to Australia.

BUR DUBAI AREA

Dubai Museum (Al Fahidi Fort)

Right in the heart of Bur Dubai lies the quaint **Al Fahidi Fort ❶** now home to Dubai Museum. This is the oldest surviving structure in the city, built between 1787 and 1799 to guard the landward approach to town. The fortress originally served as the ruler's residence and seat of government; it also provided a refuge for Dubai's inhabitants in the event of attack, whilst also serving as the city jail. The building itself – a simple, square, high-walled compound with corner towers covered in sun-baked plaster – is an arresting, if rather care-worn, sight among the surrounding modern apartment blocks and office buildings. On the square beside it stands a stunning replica of the wooden pearling *dhows* that were used in the 18th and 19th centuries.

Since 1971, the fort has housed the **Dubai Museum** (www.dubaiculture.gov. ae/en; Sat–Thu 8.30am–8.30pm, Fri 2.30–8.30pm). A visit to the museum is rewarding; most of the exhibits are displayed in a sequence of underground galleries, with excellent displays covering every aspect of traditional life in the city including an old-fashioned souk, complete with life-size shops and mannequins, plus extensive finds from the archaeological sites at Al Qusais and

Jumeira, dating back to the Iron Age and 6th century.

Juma Grand Mosque

Immediately behind the museum stands the **Juma Grand Mosque** ❷ (closed to non-Muslims). This is one of the oldest mosques in Dubai (dating back to 1900, although it was rebuilt in 1998), and also boasts the city's tallest minaret (70m/231ft), nine large domes, 45 small domes and space for 1,200 worshippers. You can take a peek inside from the doorway, but, unless you are a Muslim, don't venture in.

At the end of the souk, behind the Grand Mosque, lies the narrow alleyway known as '**Hindi Lane**' ❸, with shops selling Indian religious paraphernalia – flower garlands, portraits and horoscopes – and a tiny Hindu-cum-Sikh temple halfway along (up the stairs).

Textile Souk (Bur Dubai Old Souk)

After Hindi Lane, heading down any of the various little alleyways brings you to

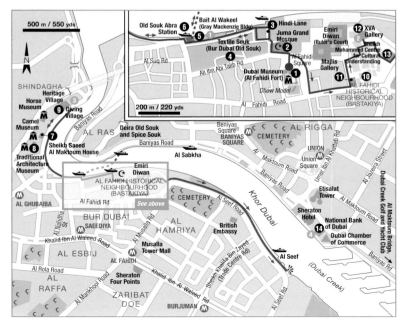

Shopping in the Textile Souk

the **Textile Souk** ❹ (Sat–Thu 10am–1pm, 4–10pm, Fri 4–10pm). This is the most attractive of all Dubai's souks, with dozens of little shops lined up in old coral-and-stone buildings under a high wooden roof; most sell cheap clothes – such as custom-made suits – and other textiles, while a few offer souvenirs and some antique handicrafts. Here and there the shops open up to reveal glorious views of the Creek, dotted with chuntering *abras* and old wooden *dhows*, with the wind-towered souks of Deira beyond.

Gray Mackenzie Building

Overlooking the *abra* station is the old, two-storey **Gray Mackenzie Building** ❺ (also known as the 'Bait Al Wakeel'), constructed in 1932. This, the first purpose-built office building in Dubai, was the initial base for the city's British agencies and trade missions. It now houses **Bait Al Wakeel**, see ❶, an Arabic restaurant overhanging the creek.

This offers a good place for lunch. Or alternatively, you can retrace your steps past the museum to the Al Fahidi Historical Neighbourhood (see page 32) and afterwards, stroll along the creekside, then take a taxi to catch up with the route for the rest of the afternoon and early evening from the *abra* station.

Dubai Old Souk Abra Station

Right next to the western entrance of the Textile Souk lies the **Old Souk Abra Station** ❻, which links up with Al Sabkha Abra Station (see page 38) in Deira. This is a hive of activity most days, with dozens of small boats jostling for custom at the pontoons.

ABRA RIDE

While you're here, it's worth hopping aboard an *abra* at the station and making the wonderful five-minute ride across the Creek. This costs just one *dirham* per person per trip, but could well be one of the highlights of your visit to Dubai. The views from the water of both sides of the Creek are magnificent – a wonderful blend of traditional and modern, with wind towers and minarets jostling for elbow room with glass-fronted high-rises and huge neon signs. The boat ride itself is equally memorable, scrunched up almost at water level amid a cosmopolitan crowd of fellow passengers who usually offer a good cross-section of Dubai society, from Pakistani expat labourers through to robed Emiratis and tanned tourists. You can either just take the next *abra* straight back, or go ashore for some exploring on the Deira route (see page 35), saving the second half of the Bur Dubai for another afternoon/evening.

SHINDAGHA

Continuing past the *abra* station, a breezy promenade leads along the waterfront into the historic district of Shindagha, with stunning views 'up-river'

Sheikh Saeed Al Maktoum House

towards the *abra* stations and the jumble of creek-side buildings and minarets.

It was here, too, that 800 members of the Al Bu Falasah sub-section of the Bani Yas tribe settled after seceding from Abu Dhabi in 1833. Led by Sheikh Maktoum Bin Buti and Sheikh Obaid Bin Saeed Bin Rashid, the Bani Yas influx transformed the politics of a community that had numbered around 1,200 people before their arrival. Maktoum became its new ruler, establishing at Shindagha the Al Maktoum dynasty that rules Dubai to this day.

Sheikh Saeed Al Maktoum House

A 5–10 minute walk brings you to **Sheikh Saeed Al Maktoum House** ❼ (www.dubaiculture.ae/en; Sat–Thu 8am–8.30pm; Fri 3–9.30pm). The former home of the ruling Maktoum family, the house was built in 1896 for Sheikh Maktoum Bin Hasher Al Maktoum, but is now named after his successor Sheikh Saeed, who ruled the emirate from 1912 to 1958. Comprehensively restored between 1984 and 1986, this two-storey structure, built from coral stone and covered in lime and sand-coloured plaster, is an impressive example of late 19th-century Emirati architecture, with elegant arched doorways, carved trellis and four wind towers.

The house is now home to one of Dubai's most interesting museums, documenting the social, cultural, educational and religious history of the emirate, although the undoubted high-

light is the fascinating collection of old photographs from the 1940s to 1960s charting the city's transformation from modest town to modern metropolis.

Traditional Architecture, Horse and Camel museums

Immediately to the south, the **Traditional Architecture Museum** ❽ (daily 7am–7pm, closed Fri; free), occupies another fine old wind-tower house, with interesting displays on architecture

---

A dynamic dynasty

Dubai's growth from the late 1950s to the present day is due mainly to Sheikh Rashid Bin Saeed Al Maktoum and his son Sheikh Mohammed. Sheikh Rashid, 'the Father of Dubai,' ruled from 1958 to 1990, building up the city's infrastructure to ensure that Dubai was well set up to exploit oil wealth when it finally came. When he died in 1990, his eldest son Sheikh Maktoum became ruler, but it was Sheikh Mohammed, younger son and Crown Prince, who was the new driving force behind the city's rapid development, leading the push towards a more diversified economy. Sheikh Maktoum died in 2006, and now 'Sheikh Mo' (as he is affectionately called, privately, by some of Dubai's residents), rules the emirate. Revered and respected by Emiratis, he can occasionally be spotted driving around in his white Mercedes 4x4 with the number plate '1'.

An Emirati man walks through the narrow streets of Al Fahidi Historical Neighbourhood

in the Emirates. Hidden away directly behind Sheikh Saeed Al Maktoum House, the modest **Camel Museum** (Sat–Thu 8am–8pm, Fri 2–8pm; free) and **Horse Museum** (daily except Fri 8am–2pm; free) are of considerably less interest, although the exhibits on camel racing in the former – including a creaking pair of animatronic dromedaries – are worth a quick look. For more details on all these museums, see www.dubaiculture.gov.ae/en.

Heritage and Diving Villages

Further north, towards the mouth of the Creek, the **Heritage Village** ❾ (www.dubaiculture.gov.ae/en; Sat–Thu 8am–10pm, Fri 3–10pm, later during festivals; free) comprises a walled compound with traditional buildings arranged around a large sandy courtyard. It's usually fairly deserted during the day, but comes to life at dusk (particularly during the winter and local festivals) with souvenir shops, food stalls (often run by local Emirati women) and occasional cultural performances. The **Diving Village** (www.dubaiculture.gov.ae/en; same hours as above; free) next door is similar, but smaller.

AL FAHIDI HISTORICAL NEIGHBOURHOOD

Retrace your steps back along the Creek and through the souk to Dubai Museum (no hardship, given the cooling sea breezes and wonderful views). Just beyond the museum along Al Fahidi Road,

on your left, you'll see the **Al Fahidi Historical Neighbourhood** ❿ (previously known as the **Bastakiya** quarter) built in the early 1900s by merchants from Bastak in southern Iran (hence the name). This is the best-preserved traditional quarter in the city: a small but surprisingly disorientating labyrinth of narrow alleyways, flanked with tall, coral-and-limestone houses topped with dozens of wind towers. These were first introduced to Dubai by Iranian settlers, but have now become synonymous with the UAE. An early form of air conditioning, these square towers capture cool air and funnel it down into the houses below, while also allowing hot air to rise and escape.

The walls of each house were made of coral stone, which, thanks to its porous nature, has low thermal conductivity, keeping temperatures inside to a minimum. For privacy and security, there were no windows on the ground floor, just a few ventilation holes. Most of the houses are fairly plain from the outside but surprisingly ornate within, usually with spacious inner courtyards, shaded with trees and surrounded by arches and doorways. A number of heritage buildings have been opened as little museums (all free), giving you the chance to have a look inside, while others have been converted into small galleries, shops, cafes and restaurants, and even a hotel.

Majlis Gallery

Right next to the entrance to the quarter, the **Majlis Gallery** ⓫ (www.themajlis

gallery.com; Sat–Thu 10am–6pm; free) is the oldest in the city, established in 1976 to showcase the work of UAE artists, as well as international artists with UAE ties. The gallery also sells traditional craft items, such as curved *khanjars* (traditional daggers worn by UAE nationals until the 1970s and still worn by men in neighbouring Oman), goatskin water bags and jewellery.

XVA Gallery

On the opposite side of Bastakiya, the **XVA Gallery** ⑫ (www.xvagallery.com; daily 10am–6pm; free) puts on shows of contemporary work from across the Middle East, and also has a lovely courtyard **coffee shop**, see ②, plus atmospheric accommodation in traditional rooms in one of Dubai's rare boutique hotels (see page 102).

Sheikh Mohammed Centre

On the eastern side of the area, in yet another traditional building, the **Sheikh Mohammed Centre for Cultural Understanding** ⑬ (www.cultures.ae; Sun–Thu 9am–5pm, Sat 9am–1pm, Fri closed; free, except tours and lunch) was created to foster awareness and understanding of local Emirati culture – over 90 percent of Dubai's population are expatriates, and it's quite possible to spend long periods in the city without meeting a single UAE national. The centre is a non-profit-making organisation, established by and named after Dubai's ruler, which promotes mutual under-standing among people from different cultures. Activities include walking tours of the district, guided tours of Jumeira Mosque and 'cultural lunches', during which you can meet local Emiratis over a traditional meal.

BUR DUBAI CREEKSIDE

Southeast of the Bastakiya district, you can continue walking along beside the Creek – looking back, there are fine views of the clustered wind towers of Al Fahidi and the tall white minaret of the mosque in the grounds of the **Emiri Diwan**, or Ruler's Court. Continuing down the promenade you'll pass the large cemetery on your right which once marked the edge of the old town, while along the waterfront fishermen still wait for *sheirii, safi, neiser* and catfish to bite.

About 1km south of Al Fahidi Neighbourhood, past the British Embassy, a superb cluster of modern buildings can be seen rising up across on the Deira side of the Creek. Particularly striking is the **National Bank of Dubai** ⑭ (1998), designed by Carlos Ott with a vast convex glass front shaped like a sail. The glassy façade reflects the water and the passing river traffic; it's particularly dramatic towards dusk, when it seems to be ablaze with the light of the setting sun.

To the right of the National Bank of Dubai stands the minimalist blue glass wedge of the **Dubai Chamber of Commerce** building. To the left stands the **Sheraton Hotel**, one of the oldest in

From left to right: Arbift Tower, Al Reem Tower, Etisalat Tower 1 and Dubai Creek Tower Deira

Dubai, with its triangular façade a little like a ship's prow jutting out into the water. Behind the Sheraton you'll notice the **Etisalat Tower**, the headquarters for Dubai's first telecommunications company, and instantly recognisable thanks to the enormous 'golf ball'-like structure on its roof.

Further right, **Al Maktoum Bridge** is one of four bridges that cross the Creek (the other three are further inland) and, just visible behind that, the distinctive roof of the **Dubai Creek Golf & Yacht Club**. From here, it's a short taxi ride back to Bur Dubai and Shindagha, where you'll find many great places for an evening meal, such as **Kan Zaman**, see ③. Alternatively, Bur Dubai creekside and across in Deira are home to several great options for **dinner cruises**, see ④.

Food and drink

① BAIT AL WAKEEL

Bur Dubai Old Souk tel: 04 353 0530; daily noon–10pm; $$

In the old Gray Mackenzie Building, seating is either inside the attractively restored period interior or outside on the deck overlooking all the action on the Creek. Service is relaxed, but a decent range of well-prepared mezze plus a few other options make it good for either lunch or dinner.

② XVA GALLERY

Al Fahidi Historical Neighbourhood; tel: 04 353 5383; www.xvahotel.com; Sat–Thu 7am–9pm; $$

Delightful courtyard café in a historic house that is now an art gallery and boutique hotel. The café is one of Dubai's best 'hidden gems' and offers a fresh and healthy menu of vegetarian fare including salads, soups, sandwiches and fruit juices, making it perfect for a refreshing lunch.

③ KAN ZAMAN

Creekside, Shindagha; tel: 04 393 9913; daily 6pm–1.30am; $

In a fine location near the Heritage Village at the mouth of the Creek, Kan Zaman has breezy outdoor and waterside seating and a good selection of Lebanese mezze, some Emirati dishes, Turkish coffee and shisha pipes. A great place for dinner to round off your day in Bur Dubai.

④ DINNER CRUISES

Most tour operators offer dhow dinner cruises along the Creek aboard various vessels (see page 128). Two of the most popular are the traditional Al Mansour Dhow operated by the Radisson Blu hotel in Deira (tel: 04 205 7333) and the more contemporary Bateaux Dubai (tel: 04 399 4994; www.jebelali-international.com). The Danat Dubai (tel: 04 351 1117; www.danat dubaicruises.com), a modern sightseeing and dining boat, is anchored at the junction of Al Seef Road and Sheikh Khalifa Bin Zayed/Trade Centre Road. The same company offers a more sedate ride aboard a wooden *dhow*.

Al Ahmadiya School

DEIRA

This leisurely day-long walking route offers a rewarding wander around Deira's souks, while a couple of absorbing heritage buildings and a visit to the city's old wooden dhow anchorage round out the tour, before ending with cocktails at the Boardwalk.

DISTANCE: 6km (3.7 miles)
TIME: A full day
START: Gold Souk
END: Dubai Creek Golf & Yacht Club
POINTS TO NOTE: To reach the starting point of the route, either take a taxi directly to the Gold Souk or a taxi to Bur Dubai Abra Station and then an *abra* to Deira Old Souk Abra Station, from where it's just a few minutes walk to the Gold Souk. At the very end of the tour you'll probably want to take a taxi from the southern *dhow* moorings to the Dubai Creek Golf & Yacht Club – this should cost only around Dhs10.

The commercial heart of the old city, life in Deira still largely revolves around the souk. The shops may be largely modern, and jazzy neon signs may have replaced the traditional hand-painted boards, but business here is still conducted more or less as it has been for over a century past, with thousands of shoebox shops wedged into the district's rambling bazaars, retailing everything from cheap toys and tex-tiles through to gold and frankincense – a far cry from the modern malls which dominate newer parts of Dubai.

The district is also home to a number of other rewarding heritage sights, including the fine old Al Ahmadiya School and adjacent Heritage House, plus the memorable *dhow* moorings, with dozens of old-fashioned Arabian *dhows* tied up along the banks of the Creek, as well as more modern sights on the creek side such as the towering buildings, relaxing hotels, and the sails of the Dubai Creek Golf & Yacht Club.

Before the shopping starts, ease yourself into the day by first heading to Al Ahmadiya Street to visit Al Ahmadiya School and the Heritage House, a pair of neatly restored traditional buildings now housing low-key museums and offering fascinating glimpses of life in old Dubai.

AL AHMADIYA SCHOOL

Established in 1912 by local pearl merchant Ahmad Bin Dalmouk (after whom it's named), **Al Ahmadiya School** ❶ (Al

A Heritage House exhibit

Ahmadiya Street; www.dubaiculture.gov.ae/en; 8am–7.30pm, Fri 2.30–7.30pm; free) was the first semi-formal school in Dubai.

Built in three phases, Al Ahmadiya School was initially a single-storey structure with 11 classrooms and a *liwan*, or veranda, around an inner courtyard, while the upper floor was added in 1920. In 1932, following the collapse of the pearl trade – and with it the local economy – the school was forced to close, but it reopened in 1937 with a govern-ment subsidy. In 1956, with the introduction of a formal education system for boys (1958 for girls), student numbers increased, and, by 1962, the school had 823 students – more than it could comfortably accommodate. In 1963, the school moved to a new, larger site, and the original building was closed. Illustrious alumni include Sheikh Rashid Bin Saeed Al Maktoum, 'the Father of Dubai', who worked relentlessly to modernise the city as ruler between 1958 and 1990, and Sheikh Mohammed Bin

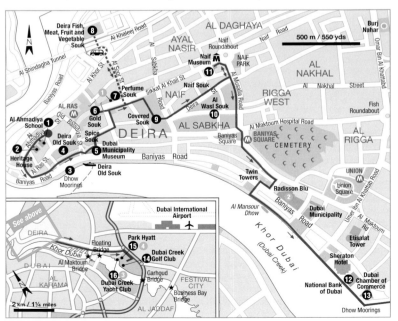

Dhow cargo boats moored at Dubai Creek

Rashid Al Maktoum, UAE vice president, prime minister and ruler of Dubai.

By the mid 1990s, the building had become completely derelict and was in danger of collapsing completely until being meticulously restored by the Dubai Municipality's Historical Buildings Section using authentic building materials such as coral stone, gypsum and sandalwood. Like most of Dubai's traditional buildings, the decorative doorway opens into a courtyard, or *al housh*, surrounded by verandas and various rooms. The courtyard was the place where school assemblies were held and where pupils did their exercises and had their breaks.

The rooms around the courtyard now house some low-key exhibits covering the history of the school, including mannequins of pupils in traditional dress. There are more classrooms upstairs, still equipped with their old wooden desks and chairs.

HERITAGE HOUSE

Next to Al Ahmadiya School is the **Heritage House** ❷ (www.dubaiculture. gov.ae/en; Sat–Thu 8am–7.30pm, Fri 2.30–7.30pm; free). Originally built in 1890 for Mohammed Bin Saeed Bin Muzaaina, it was subsequently acquired in 1910 by pearl trader Ahmad Bin Dalmouk, who expanded the house, as well as establishing the school next door. Like Al Ahmadiya School, the Heritage House was also restored in the mid-

1990s and opened to the public in 2000 as a reminder of the city's pre-oil era.

Today, the 935 sq m (10,065 sq ft) building is preserved as it would have been in the 1940s and 1950s. This is one of best surviving examples of a traditional Emirati home, providing an atmospheric snapshot of the social life of Dubai's wealthier inhabitants during that period. Notable features include the separate men's and women's *majlis*, or meeting rooms, where guests would have sat on embroidered pillows around the edge of a Persian-carpeted floor.

DHOW MOORINGS

Turn left out of the Heritage House and follow the road around to reach Baniyas Road running alongside the Creek, then turn left again along the waterfront until you reach Deira Old Souk Abra Station after a couple more minutes. Facing the Creek on your left is the warren of lanes and alleyways that make up Deira Old Souk. Ahead of you, stretching down the waterfront, are the old city's **dhow moorings** ❸, with lines of traditional old wooden cargo boats moored up along the edge of the Creek – an unexpectedly old-fashioned sight amongst the modern traffic and office blocks.

Huge piles of cargo usually stand stacked up along the road here – anything from mounds of fizzy drinks to washing machines and the occasional car – waiting to be loaded up onto boats and shipped off overseas. Many of the

Colours and smells galore in the Spice Souk

dhows here head off to Iran (and many have Iranian crews). The impossibility of enforcing proper customs procedures along the crowded roadside has proved something of a headache for the authorities; attempts are being made to gradually move shipping to more secure facilities down the coast. For the time being, however, the *dhows* remain.

DEIRA OLD SOUK

Turning away from the Creek, head into the attractive tangle of covered alleyways making up **Deira Old Souk** ❹ (most shops open Sat–Thu 10am–10pm – although some close between around 1–4pm – and Fri 4–10pm). Most of the souk's shops are now devoted to relatively mundane items like cheap toys, textiles and clothing.

The most interesting part of the Old Souk is the **Spice Souk**, close to Deira Old Souk Abra Station. This is one of the prettiest corners of Deira, a few narrow alleyways with shops fronted by colourful sacks and trays of fragrant produce, although unfortunately it's also shrinking due to competition from local hypermarkets and supermarkets, which is where most modern Dubaians now go for their spices. Goods on offer include mainstream spices (plus relatively inexpensive saffron) and other local cooking ingredients like dried cucumbers and lemons, as well as piles of rose petals, used to scent tea. The souk is also a good place to buy frankincense, sold in various different forms and grades; frankincense burners can also be bought in the souk for a few dirhams. Most stalls also sell natural cosmetic products such as pumice and *alum*, a clear rock crystal used as a kind of mineral aftershave.

Right in front of the Spice Souk (opposite Deira Old Souk Abra Station) stands the small **Dubai Municipality Museum** ❺ (www.dm.gov.ae; Sat–Thu 8am–2pm, during Ramadan 9am–5pm; free), occupying the former headquarters of the Dubai Municipality – a simple but elegant, two-storey structure with a long wooden balcony offering fine views over the commercial hustle and bustle below. Inside, the museum hosts a modern array of civic documents and old photographs.

GOLD SOUK

From here, you're a short walk away up 'Souk Street' to the entrance for the **Gold Souk** ❻ (most shops open Sat–Thu 10am–10pm – although some close between around 1–4pm – and Fri 4–10pm), probably the most famous in Dubai, and certainly the most valuable. There are about a hundred shops here, lined up under a wooden roof, their windows overflowing with vast quantities of gold jewellery ranging from florid Arabian designs through to more understated pieces – the traditional Emirati-style bracelets are particularly nice.

Dubai is one of the cheapest places in the world to buy gold, attracting a colourful array of shoppers from West

Gold Souk wares   *Fragrance from the Perfume Souk*

Africa, Russia, India and elsewhere. Jewellery is sold by weight (despite its intricacy, the quality of the workmanship isn't usually factored into the price). If you ask the price of an item, it will first be put on the scales and weighed, and its value calculated according to the day's gold price (which may be displayed in the shop). Asking for 'discount' or 'special price' should help knock a further chunk off the price. At this point – and assuming you're still interested in buying the piece – it's time to start bargaining. If you are interested in buying something, do not reveal your full interest to the seller. Start your offer low – at around half the amount you estimate you would finally like to spend.

Many shops also sell silver and precious stones, while the area is also a major centre for Dubai's thriving trade in designer fakes.

PERFUME SOUK

Returning to the Gold Souk entrance, head east for a block along Sikkat Al Khail Street and then turn left up Al Soor Street. Dozens of traditional perfume shops line these two streets, an area commonly known as the **Perfume Souk** ❼ (most shops open Sat–Thu 10am–10pm – although some close between around 1–4pm – and Fri 4–10pm). Shops stock a mix of western brands (not necessarily genuine) and more flowery local scents. Many places can also mix up a bespoke perfume for you on request from the rows of glass scent bottles lined up behind the counters.

FISH, MEAT, FRUIT AND VEG

Continue to the top of Al Soor Street and across the Gold Souk Bus Station

Traditional Emirati houses

Traditional houses along the Gulf coast were built from locally available materials – usually pieces of coral stone bound together with pounded gypsum, with roofs made out of mangrove wood (or, in grander residences, Indian teak). The emphasis was on privacy and security: most houses have few windows and usually only one entrance. Inside, most dwellings were centred on large interior courtyards, providing space for children to play and livestock to graze. The *majlis* (meeting room) is another standard feature (plus, in larger establishments, a dedicated ladies' *majlis* as well). Traditional houses were remarkably well adapted to their environment in the days before air-conditioning. The thick walls and smallness of windows both helped keep interiors cool, while wind towers captured any passing breezes and funnelled them down to the rooms below. Houses were also built close together, helping to create narrow and almost permanently shaded alleyways between.

The vast Fish Souk

on the far side of which a footbridge crosses the busy Al Khaleej Road to reach the **Fish, Meat, Fruit and Vegetable Souk** ❽, the old city's main wholesale area for all things edible. Before venturing inside, take time to wander among the ice lorries parked to the right of the main building. The fish are kept here in iceboxes and either wheeled into the market by porters or sold to bulk buyers such as restaurateurs. You'll be amazed at the variety of shapes and sizes of fish, and, here in the sun, you can also appreciate their often stunning colours. Red snappers, belt fish, kingfish, sardines and baby sharks are among those weighed and tossed into barrows or flat-bed trucks. In the market proper, walk between the trays of fish towards the sound of chopping at the top left of the hall. Here, buyers can have their fish descaled, filleted and diced by an army of knife-wielding workers in blue overalls.

Next to the fish souk – but definitely not for those of a squeamish disposition – is the smaller **Meat Souk**, where skinned goats (the carcasses come complete with tails), lambs (without tails) and cows hang. Somewhat easier on both the nose and the eye is the **Fruit and Vegetable Souk** in the next hall, a particularly good place to buy a wide range of dates from across the Gulf.

Assuming the sight of all this food has made you hungry, return down Al Soor Street for a classic Dubai lunch of *shawarma* at the small but enduringly popular **Ashwaq**, see ❶, a no-frills little cafeteria whose pavement tables are one of the best places in Deira to people-watch.

THE COVERED SOUK

Continue east along Sikkat Al Khail Road back past the junction with Al Soor St, then turn right down any of the various little lanes to reach the **Covered Souk** ❾ (most shops open Sat–Thu 10am–10pm – although some close between around 1–4pm – and Fri 4–10pm). The shops and merchandise here are fairly humdrum compared to other souks in Deira – household items, cheap toys and clothes predominate – although it's an enjoyable area for an aimless and disorientating wander, attempting to pick a route between the shops and piles of merchandise through the labyrinth of tiny lanes and alleyways.

AL WASI SOUK

Keep heading east and, all being well, you'll come out somewhere along Al Sabkha Road. Cross this and continue through **Al Wasl Souk** ❿ – even bigger and more disorientating, particularly after dark, when the pavements are thronged with crowds of local shoppers. There are all sorts of different routes through the bazaar, although it's more fun to wander where the urge

A Deira street scene

takes you, aiming ultimately to come out around the northeastern corner of the souk somewhere near the junction of Sikkat Al Khail Street and Al Musalla Road.

NAIF MUSEUM

At the far eastern end of Sikkat Al Khail Street, close to the junction with Al Musalla Road, stands the interesting, but little-visited **Naif Museum** ⓫ (www.dubaiculture.gov.ae/en; Sat–Thu 8am–2pm; free) in **Naif Fort**, the first headquarters of Dubai Police, when the force was established by Sheikh Rashid in 1956.

The fort, which remains a police station today, was added to a single square defensive tower constructed in 1939 to bolster the defence of the northern approach to Dubai. The original tower still stands, while the rest of the fort was reconstructed in 1994 on the orders of Sheikh Mohammed (himself a former head of Dubai Police and Public Security in 1968, a position to which he was appointed at the age of just 19).

The museum is housed in a room below the tower. Among the exhibits are early handguns and rifles, a stock restraint, known as Al Hataba, for prisoners' feet, and uniforms, including the current military-style green outfit and the first police *kandoura*, which was white with a red belt and red epaulettes.

SOUTH ALONG THE CREEK

From the Naif Museum it's a 10-minute walk down busy Al Musalla Road to Baniyas Square, the centre of modern Deira, then onto the Creek. A wide and attractive waterfront walkway heads south from here, running past the Radisson Blu hotel (formerly the InterContinental, the city's first five-star when it opened in 1970) and a line of tourist *dhows* moored up along the waterfront.

The Radisson Blu has a number of good venues for lunch or dinner, including **Yum!**, see ❷, and Shabestan (see page 109).There are fine views back up the Creek towards the city centre from here, with the wind towers of the Al Fahidi Historical Neighbourhood over the water in Bur Dubai.

A leisurely 10-minute stroll brings you to the cluster of modernist creekside buildings which you may already have seen from the Bur Dubai side of the water (see page 33), including the landmark **National Bank of Dubai building** ⓬ and the triangular-topped **Dubai Chamber of Commerce** ⓭, as well as the Sheraton Hotel, and the Etisalat Tower, surmounted by its distinctive 'golf ball'.

Immediately south of the Dubai Chamber of Commerce, a second set of *dhow* moorings line the banks of the Creek, and are usually home to dozens more traditional wooden *dhows*, surreally framed by the glass-fronted modernist buildings behind.

Dubai Creek Golf Club

DUBAI CREEK GOLF & YACHT CLUB

The southern end of the *dhow* moorings is marked by Maktoum Bridge, the first in the city when it was opened in 1963. Beyond here stretches the expansive grounds of the beautiful **Dubai Creek Golf Club** ⑭ (although it's not much fun walking down the busy Baniyas Road, so get a cab – around Dhs10).

The club is best known for its famous clubhouse, an eye-catching structure inspired by the triangular sails of the traditional Arabian *dhow* and looking a bit like a Dubai version of the Sydney Opera House in miniature. Close by stands the idyllic **Park Hyatt** hotel ⑮,

with its pretty, rather Moorish-looking swathe of white-walled, blue-domed buildings overlooking the adjacent **Dubai Creek Yacht Club** ⑯ where dozens of expensive yachts sit moored up alongside the Creek.

There's a surprisingly good range of places to eat and drink here, either in the golf clubhouse, at the yacht club or in the Park Hyatt. The lively **Boardwalk** restaurant, see ③, offers waterfront dining at the yacht club, while The **Terrace** bar at the Park Hyatt, see ④, is particularly lovely, with sublime creekside views past the yachts and down to the high-rises of Deira in one direction, and Sheikh Zayed Road in the other.

Food and drink

① ASHWAQ

Sikkat Al Khail Road, near the entrance to the Gold Souk; daily 10am–10pm; $
A popular little cafeteria, serving up juicy *shawarma* sandwiches and big cups of various fruit juices – get your lunch then grab a seat at one of the pavement tables.

② YUM!

Radisson Blu, Dubai Deira Creek; tel: 04 205 7033, www.radissonblu.com; daily noon–11.30pm; $$
Attractive modern noodle bar with brisk service and flavoursome pan-Asian dishes – mainly Thai, plus a few Chinese, Malay, Indonesian and Singaporean dishes.

③ THE BOARDWALK

Dubai Creek Golf & Yacht Club; tel: 04 295 6000; www.dubaigolf.com; Sun–Thu noon–midnight, Fri and Sat 8am–midnight; $$
The menu of international food is reliable enough, but it's the terrific Creek and city views from the outdoor seating that really steal the show.

④ THE TERRACE PARK HYATT HOTEL

Park Hyatt Hotel, nr Dubai Creek Golf & Yacht Club; tel: 04 602 1814; www.dubai.park. hyatt.com; $$$
A very smooth Creekside cocktail bar, with a superior (if pricey) drinks list, discreet ambient music and wonderful waterside views.

Children's City building in Creekside Park

OUD METHA, UMM HURAIR, KARAMA AND SATWA

This route threads its way from Dubai Creek through the suburbs dividing the old city centre from the more upmarket, high-rise districts further south – a part of Dubai often missed by visitors, although there are many attractions tucked away here.

DISTANCE: 9km (5.5 miles)
TIME: A full day
START: Creekside Park, Oud Metha
END: 2nd December Street (formerly Al Diyafah Street), Satwa
POINTS TO NOTE: Take a taxi to Creekside Park, and then continue on foot or catch another cab to Wafi. From here, its another taxi for the short journey to Karama souk, followed by a third cab from Karama for the quick ride across to Satwa. If you start the tour mid-morning, you can aim to have lunch either in Wafi or adjacent Khan Murjan and then continue over to Karama towards dusk before heading over to Satwa for an evening meal and a chance to sample the after-dark streetlife of one of Dubai's most vibrant areas.

In contrast to the newer suburbs of Jumeirah Beach Residence and Downtown Dubai, this part of the city is less pristine, with a charmingly rugged edge that is a welcome break from the immaculately designed expat havens. Explore Oud Metha and Umm Hurair, before continuing to bustling Karama and Satwa, two of the city's oldest and most personable working-class districts.

OUD METHA AND UMM HURAIR

South of Bur Dubai, this district is something of a hotchpotch – rather lacking in character or streetlife, but home to some of the inner-city's biggest tourist developments, including the spectacular Wafi City complex and the adjacent Raffles hotel and Khan Murjan souk.

Creekside Park

Stretching south, and inland, from the Maktoum Bridge, the spacious **Creekside Park ❶** (aka Creek Park; www.dm.gov.ae; Sun–Wed 8am–10pm, Thu–Sat until 11.00pm) offers one of the few sizeable open areas in the congested city centre. It's a pleasant place for a stroll in nicely landscaped gardens, with plenty of trees providing some shady walks, and has fine views over the Creek to the quaint buildings

Take a ride on the Dubai Creek Cable Car

of the Park Hyatt hotel and distinctive Dubai Creek Golf Club on the far side of the water. Even finer views can be had (best in the cooler months) from the rickety old cable car (Dhs25, children Dhs15), which travels the length of the park.

Children's City

The park is also home to the excellent **Children's City** ❷ (www.childrencity. dm.gov.ae; Sat–Thu 9am–8pm, Fri 3–9pm). If you've got kids in tow, this is a rewarding destination, with a fun, interactive range of galleries exploring various themes including science, nature, space exploration and cultures of the world. Even without kids, it's worth a peek at the City's striking buildings, painted in bright primary colours and looking a bit like some kind of supersized Lego construction.

Dubai Dolphinarium

Just inside the park, next to Gate #1, the **Dubai Dolphinarium** ❸ (www. dubaidolphinarium.ae) offers another fun destination for kids. The Dolphinarium stages daily shows (at 11am, 3pm & 6pm, check website for full details) featuring the centre's bottlenose dolphins and seals, with the obligatory jumping through hoops and flipping of balls. A more rewarding (and expensive) alternative is to go for a swim with the dolphins (Dhs400 for a group session; reservations required). There are also three showings daily of the Exotic Bird Show.

Wafi City

Exit Creekside Park via Gate #1 (where you might find a taxi to hail), then turn left down Riyadh Road and then right down 26th Street, around the back of

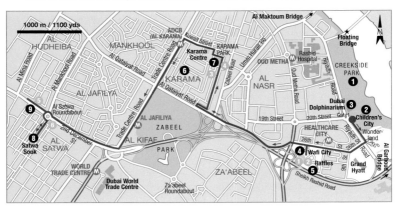

Wafi City   *Raffles Hotel*

the huge Grand Hyatt hotel, the largest in the city until the opening of Atlantis The Palm (see page 63). Turn right, again on Street 26, and you will reach the glitzy **Wafi City** ❹ complex (www.waficity.com; daily 10am–10pm, Thu & Fri until midnight). The centrepiece of Umm Hurair, Wafi looks like a little slice of Las Vegas dropped into the middle of the Gulf, with a comic-book, Egyptian-style design featuring a zany mishmash of huge pharaonic statues, hieroglyphs, spectacular stained-glass windows and half a dozen miniature pyramids dotted across the sprawling rooflines. It's cheesy but entertaining, while the complex also provides one of the city's most attractive shopping and eating destinations. **Elements** café, see ❶, is a particularly appealing spot for a light lunch or drink.

Khan Murjan

Beneath the Wafi complex is the beautiful **Khan Murjan** souk (www.wafi.com/souk-in-dubai; daily 10am–10pm, Thu & Fri until midnight), inspired by the legendary 14th-century Khan Murjan souk in Baghdad. This is one of Dubai's finest exercises in Orientalist kitsch, with virtually every available surface covered in lavishly detailed Arabian-style design featuring elaborate Moroccan-style tilework, intricately carved wooden doors and ceilings, and huge hanging lamps. The souk is home to over a hundred shops retailing all manner of upmarket Arabian (plus some

Indian) handicrafts, while the superb **Khan Murjan Restaurant**, see ❷, at the heart of the souk offers a memorable venue for lunch or dinner.

Raffles Hotel

Next door to Wafi – and continuing the Egyptian theme – the vast postmodern pyramid of **Raffles Hotel** ❺ (www.raffles.com/dubai) provides one of the city centre's most dramatic landmarks, visible for miles around and particularly impressive after dusk, when the glass-walled summit of the pyramid is lit up from within, glowing magically in the darkness. Inside, the main foyer is well worth a look, with huge Egyptian-style columns covered in lavish hieroglyph. It's also worth a visit later in the evening for a drink in the People by Crystal bar and nightclub at the very top of the pyramid, with stylish contemporary décor and sweeping city views.

From Wafi, it's a short taxi ride (around Dhs10) north to Karama Souk – it is easy to find a taxi, you'll find several lined up outside the main entrance to Wafi.

KARAMA

Karama ❻ is a hive of activity; the area is home to many of the lower-paid expats, predominately from India, Pakistan, Sri Lanka and the Philippines, who largely provide the city with its taxi drivers, waitresses, housemaids and construction workers. The area offers a

A section of Dubai Metro's elevated tracks, on the road from Karama to Sheikh Zayed Road

refreshingly different insight into life in the city away from the tourist fleshpots and sky-age architecture.

Karama Shopping Complex

The heart of this district is the busy **Karama Shopping Complex** ❼ (most shops open Sat–Thu 10am–10pm, although some close in the afternoon from around 1–4pm, Fri 4–10pm), basically a pair of open-air concrete arcades stuffed with dozens of Indian-run shops selling all manner of clothes, shoes, DVDs and household items, plus a decent range of souvenirs. The souk is best known as the epicentre for Dubai's roaring trade in designer fakes – imitation bags, watches, sunglasses and other counterfeit-branded items, as well as pirated DVDs – although following government crackdowns these are occasionally kept out of sight in backrooms behind the various shops. You won't get more than a few paces into the souk before being regaled with offers of 'cheap copy watches' and the like. The quality of many of the fakes is surprisingly high, although prices can be unexpectedly steep – if you do decide to buy, check workmanship carefully and bargain like mad.

Karama Park and Kuwait Street

Immediately north of the souk lies **Karama Park**, a small square of grass surrounded by dozens of inexpensive but generally excellent curry houses, such as **Saravana Bhavan**, see ❸, and **Karachi Darbar**, see ❹. Others worth trying include Chef Lanka, Aryaas and Paratha King. This is the social heart of the suburb, usually busy with crowds of strolling residents in the afternoons and evenings.

Turn west (left) at the end of the park to reach Kuwait Street, Karama's main thoroughfare, where you'll find the modest Karama Centre, home to some interesting little shops selling a colourful selection of richly embroidered saris and *salwar kameez*. The whole strip is particularly lively after dark.

SATWA

From Kuwait Street, catch a taxi for the short ride (roughly Dhs10) to the Satwa Roundabout, at the heart of the neighbouring suburb of Satwa. South of the roundabout is **Satwa Souk** ❽, a hub for the district's Indian community, with an engaging string of low-key shops and a forest of neon signs.

Retrace your steps to Satwa Roundabout and then head west along **2nd December Street** (formerly **Al Diyafah Street**) ❾, Satwa's de facto high street. This is one of the most pleasant places in the city to take a stroll after dark, with broad, tree-lined pavements dotted with a long string of cafés and restaurants, including several excellent Lebanese eateries. The unpretentious strip attracts a refreshingly mixed crowd of Dubai's multicultural population and locals; expats and tourists come here

View over Satwa

to stroll, people-watch from the many pavement cafés and converse – this is Dubai on a refreshingly human scale. For food, good Lebanese mezze and *shawarma* can be found at **Al Mallah**, see ⑤, on 2nd December Street, while close by, just off Satwa Roundabout, is the ever-popular **Ravi's**, see ⑥.

Food and drink

① ELEMENTS

Wafi Mall, Oud Metha; 04 324 4252; daily 10am–midnight; $$

Funky little place serving up a wide selection of reasonably priced café fare ranging from sandwiches, salads and pizzas through to dim sum and sushi, plus more substantial meat and fish mains.

② KHAN MURJAN RESTAURANT

Khan Murjan Souk, Oud Metha; daily 10am–11.30pm; $$$

Beautiful courtyard restaurant at the heart of Khan Murjan Souk. The menu features an unusually wide range of Middle Eastern dishes, from mainstream Lebanese grills and mezze through to traditional Gulf dishes like *fouga* and *goboli*.

③ SARAVANA BHAVAN

Opp Karama Park; tel: 04 334 5252, www.saravanabhavan.com; daily 7.30am–11pm, Fri closed 11.30am–1.30pm; $

Of the innumerable bargain curry houses in Dubai, this offshoot (plus six other branches) of the popular restaurant chain from Chennai is one of the best, attracting a local loyal following for its delicious, bargain-priced pure-veg South Indian cuisine. Try the thali or dosa.

④ KARACHI DARBAR

Karama, between Karama Shopping Complex and Karama Park; daily 10am–10pm; $

A long-established curry house dishing up huge portions of tasty Pakistani-style chicken or mutton curries at bargain-basement prices.

⑤ AL MALLAH

2nd December Street, Satwa; daily 10am–10pm; $

One of several good Lebanese cafés along 2nd December Street, with a good range of inexpensive Middle Eastern mezze, snacks and meals (including some of the best shawarma and falafel in town) and plenty of seating on the pavement outside – a great place to watch the nightlife of Satwa roll past.

⑥ RAVI'S

Just off Satwa Roundabout, Satwa; daily 10am–11pm; $

This legendary little café remains enduringly popular with locals, expats and tourists alike for its cheap and tasty Pakistani-style chicken, mutton and vegetable curries, while the outdoor seating offers a good (if noisy) perch from which to enjoy the passing streetlife.

SHEIKH ZAYED ROAD
AND DOWNTOWN DUBAI

This eye-catching area shows Dubai at its most brazenly futuristic and wildly ambitious, with a long string of neck-straining skyscrapers leading south towards the often cloud-capped Burj Khalifa, the world's tallest building.

DISTANCE: 5km (3.1 miles)
TIME: A full day
START: Dubai World Trade Centre
END: Downtown Dubai
POINTS TO NOTE: Exactly how long this route lasts depends largely on how much time you'd like to take on the journey from Trade Centre along Sheikh Zayed Road, and how long you plan on spending in the Dubai Mall and Downtown Dubai area. You can start late morning, allowing you a little sightseeing along Sheikh Zayed Road, and possibly dipping into the art galleries at DIFC, then finding somewhere for lunch. The afternoon could be making the rest of the way to Downtown Dubai for shopping or exploring the other leisure activities and getting up close to Burj Khalifa, then make sure you're in Downtown Dubai after nightfall for dinner, when the magnificent Dubai Fountain is at its most spectacular.

Record-breaking developments are seldom far away in this part of town, including not only the world's tallest building, but also the biggest shopping mall, largest fountain and tallest hotel. If you're looking for traditional Arabia, you've come to the wrong place. If you want extravagant sci-fi architecture and postmodern urban pizzazz, however, few other places on the planet can match this part of Dubai.

The route starts at the landmark World Trade Centre before heading south between the massed skyscrapers of Sheikh Zayed Road and then onto Downtown Dubai and the Burj Khalifa. If the weather permits, you can walk the whole route. Alternatively, if it's hot, or your feet need a rest, you can easily cut the duration of the route down by taking the metro, allowing you to stay cool while taking in the spectacular views.

SHEIKH ZAYED ROAD

Sheikh Zayed Road is one of Dubai's iconic images: a huge, twelve-lane highway flanked on either side by rows of densely packed skyscrapers, whose

The interchange at Sheikh Zayed Road lit up by traffic at dusk

towering façades create an almost unbroken wall of glass and metal, like some kind of architectural canyon. The road itself is one of the busiest in the city, part of the main highway through Dubai, and also linking it to Abu Dhabi, and is named after the first president of the UAE. Running alongside the road, the city's futuristic metro – with its distinctive pod-shaped stations – also offers fine views from its elevated track.

Dubai World Trade Centre

At the northern end of Sheikh Zayed Road, next to Trade Centre Roundabout, stands the 39-floor **Dubai World Trade Centre ❶**. Easily overlooked, this relatively modest, decidedly old-fashioned construction was actually the first high-rise in Dubai when it opened in 1979, and one of the first buildings of any kind in the Sheikh Zayed Road area, which was then largely desert. The building was widely considered an enormous white elephant at the time, but proved remarkably successful, kick-starting development in the south of the city.

From the Trade Centre, it's a 10-minute walk south to Emirates Towers. Dubai's sprawling International Convention and Exhibition Centre lies on your left, while to your right, on the far side of the road, is the distinctive **Fairmont Hotel**

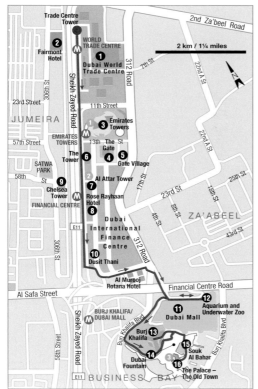

Emirates Towers lifts

❷, designed to resemble an enormous postmodern wind tower.

Emirates Towers
Standing proud above the northern end of Sheikh Zayed, the twin **Emirates Towers** ❸ were the tallest in the city upon completion in 2000, at 355m (1,165ft). They've since been outstripped many times locally , most notably, by the gargantuan Burj Khalifa just down the road, but remain two of the most distinctive, and most beautiful, modern buildings in the city, with their unusual triangular summits and huge glass and aluminium façades that appear to glow in the fierce desert light.

The larger of the two towers (off limits to the general public) houses the headquarters of Emirates airlines and the principal offices of Dubai's ruler Sheikh Mohammed and his inner circle. The smaller tower is the location for the upmarket Jumeirah Emirates Towers, the leading business hotel in the city – well worth a look for its spectacular atrium, with glass-sided elevators shuttling up and down overhead or, even better, for a drink or meal at Alta Badia restaurant or **Alta Badia Bar** (see page 110) close to the summit of the building, with peerless views over the city below. There are several other venues suitable for a lunch stop in the hotel, the upmarket Boulevard shopping mall beneath the towers (such as **The Noodle House**, see ❶), and the DIFC area.

Dubai International Financial Centre
Immediately south of the Emirates Towers stretches the **Dubai International Financial Centre (DIFC)**. The main landmark here is **The Gate** building ❹, an unusual structure resembling an office block-cum-archway, with a spacious courtyard in its centre. The building is home to the Dubai Stock Exchange, while the adjacent Gate Village complex is home to a number of upmarket art galleries. As a popular lunch venue for the businesses nearby, the area also offers some top-class dining options.

Art galleries at the DIFC
The DIFC complex provides a rather unlikely home to a surprisingly good range of galleries, in **Gate Village** ❺, which serves as one of the leading hubs of the city's burgeoning visual arts scene. Top venues include **Artspace** (Bldg No. 3, Level 2; www.artspace-dubai.com; Sun–Thu, 10am–6pm), dedicated to contemporary Middle Eastern painters and sculptures; **Cuadro Fine Art Gallery** (Building No. 10; www.cuadroart.com; Sun–Thu 10am–8pm, Sat 12am–6pm), which has a slightly more international flavour, although again with a strong Middle East emphasis; **Rira Gallery** (Bldg No. 3; http://riragallery.com; Sun–Thu 10am-8pm, Sat 12–6pm). for more Middle Eastern art; and **The Empty Quarter** (Bldg No. 3; www.theemptyquarter.com; Sun–Thu 9am–7pm) for photographic art.

The Gate   *Shadows cast by towers on Sheikh Zayed Road*

South along Sheikh Zayed Road

Continuing south along Sheikh Zayed Road, either on foot, in a cab or peering out of the Dubai Metro, you will get more views on either side of the long string of elongated skyscrapers packed in side by side. The buildings here offer a comprehensive compendium of Dubai's archetypal modern design, ranging from the functional through to the quirky and the downright bizarre.

Notable buildings along the east side of the road include **The Tower ❻**, an attractive structure topped with a pyramidal summit; the **Al Attar Tower ❼**, its plain plate-glass walls edged with enormous golden discs; and the elegant **Rose Rayhaan** hotel **❽** (the second tallest hotel in the world, at 333m (1,093ft) having lost the record to the JW Marriott Marquis Dubai in Downtown Dubai), a soaring, pencil thin edifice topped with a small globe which lights up at night. Opposite the Rose Rayhaan, on the west side of the road, stands the massive **Chelsea Tower ❾**, its summit adorned with what looks like an enormous toothpick. Further south, at the end of the strip, is perhaps the most distinctive building of them all, the **Dusit Thani hotel ❿**, a bow-legged colossus inspired by the shape of the traditional Thai *wai*, a prayer-like gesture of welcome. Located in Al Saqr Tower, the **Shakespeare & Co**. café, see ❷, is a great place for a drink or light lunch.

DOWNTOWN DUBAI

Continuing past the Dusit Thani hotel, turn left down the side road which winds around past the Al Murooj Rotana hotel (home to the cool More café, see page 111) and brings you out, after about a five minute walk, on to Financial Centre Road, opposite the main entrance to The Dubai Mall. This is part of the massive Downtown Dubai development opened in 2010 and built at an estimated cost of a cool $20 billion. The development features a string of attractions, which – in true Dubai style – all have record-breaking claims, including The Dubai Mall itself (the world's largest), along with the world's biggest fountain and, most notably, its tallest building, the sky-high Burj Khalifa.

The Dubai Mall

Shopping opportunities don't come much bigger than the gargantuan **The Dubai Mall ⓫** (www.thedubaimall.com; daily 10am–10pm, Thu–Sat until midnight). The entire complex covers a total area of over 1,100,000 sq metres (12 million sq ft), with over 1,200 shops spread across four floors, making it impressively vast and a fantastic retail experience; even if the sheer size of the place can make a shopping trip here feel a bit like a long-distance hike.

Flagship outlets include branches of the famous Galleries Lafayette and Bloomingdales department stores, a huge branch of the Japanese book-

Crowds in Dubai Aquarium

seller Kinokuniya and an offshoot of London's famous Hamleys toy store. There's also a vast selection of upmarket designer stores, mainly concentrated along 'Fashion Avenue', complete with its own catwalk, an Armani café, and a stunning Gold Souk decorated in an attractive Arabian design.

Shops apart, the mall also boasts a host of other leisure attractions. Children will enjoy the state-of-the-art **SEGA Republic** theme park and **KidZania** educational play area which allows kids to role play in a city created just for them, while there's also an Olympic-size ice rink and the Dubai Aquarium and Underwater Zoo. The mall is also home to well over a hundred cafés and restaurants, many of them located either along the waterside terrace at the back of the mall overlooking the Dubai Fountain, or along The Grove, an attractive 'outdoor' streetscape under a retractable roof.

Dubai Aquarium

Just inside the mall's main entrance lies the **Dubai Aquarium and Underwater Zoo** 12 (www.thedubaiaquarium. com; Sun–Wed 10am–10pm, Thu–Sat 10am–midnight). Towering over the surrounding shops is the aquarium's spectacular 'viewing panel': a huge, floor-to-ceiling transparent acrylic panel showing off the extraordinary array of marine life that ranges

from sand-tiger sharks and stingrays through to colourful shoals of tiny tropical fish. You can walk through the underwater tunnel (Dhs25, children Dhs20), which leads through the middle, or even go 'diving with the sharks' (advance bookings required).

The Underwater Zoo upstairs is more likely to appeal to children than to adults, with displays themed on various types of marine habitat and featuring an array of wildlife ranging from tiny cichlids and poison-dart frogs through to otters, penguins and seals.

Burj Khalifa

Walk across the mall and go out through the rear exit from the lower-ground (LG) floor from the Star Atrium. Ahead of you stretches the large lake (where the **Dubai Fountain** is located, see page 53) and a small footbridge leading to **Old Town** (see page 54).

To begin with, however, you'll probably only have eyes for the staggering **Burj Khalifa** 13, the world's tallest building, rising up on your right. Opened in early 2010, the Burj Khalifa (828m/ 2,716ft) has obliterated all previous records for the world's tallest man-made structures, smashing the record for the world's tallest building (formerly held by Taipei 101 in Taiwan, at 509m) by a staggering 300m. The tower also holds claim to a host of other superlatives, including the building with the most floors (160), the world's highest and fastest elevators, plus highest

mosque (158th floor) and swimming pool (76th floor).

The Burj was designed by Adrian Smith of the Chicago architectural firm Skidmore, Owings and Merrill (whose other high-rise creations include the Willis Tower, formerly the Sears Tower, in Chicago; and New York's 1 World Trade Center). The simple but elegant design is based on an unusual Y-shaped ground plan, where three projecting wings are gradually stepped back as the tower rises, so that the entire building becomes progressively narrower as it gains height.

The astonishing size of the Burj Khalifa and distinctively tapering outline is hard to grasp close up – the whole thing is best appreciated from a distance, from where you can properly grasp its jaw-dropping size, and the degree to which it dwarfs the surrounding high-rises, many of which are considerable structures in their own right.

Visiting the Burj Khalifa

Much of the tower is occupied by around 900 very exclusive residential apartments, while 15 of the lower floors are given over to the world's first Armani hotel (www.armanihotels.com). The easiest way to visit the tower is to take the expensive trip to 'At the Top', the misleadingly-named observation deck (on floor 124 – there are actually 160 floors in total). Tours leave from the ticket counter on the lower-ground floor of The Dubai Mall. Tickets cost from Dhs125 if pre-booked online at www.burjkhalifa.ae or pre-purchased at the ticket counter. If you want to go up without a prior reservation, you'll have to fork out a mighty Dhs300. Make sure you book well in advance – there's usually a waiting list of a week to go up the tower.

Dubai Fountain

Lying between the Burj Khalifa and the Dubai Mall is a large lake, surrounded by attractive pedestrianised waterfront promenades. Inserted into the section of the lake closest to The Dubai Mall is the spectacular **Dubai Fountain** ❶ (www.thedubaimall.com/en/enter tain/thedubaifountain.aspx). Standing in the shadow of the world's tallest building, this is, appropriately enough, purported to be the world's largest fountain at 275 metres (900ft) long, with water canons capable of shooting choreographed jets of water up to 150 metres (490ft) high into the air which 'dance' in time to a range of Arabic, Hindi and classical music. After dark, the fountain is illuminated with over 6,000 multi-coloured lights and 25 colour projectors that play across the watery plumes. The magnificent shows are staged daily at 1pm and 1.30pm (Friday 1.30pm and 2pm), and every 30 minutes between 6pm and 11pm in the evening, and can be watched for free from anywhere around the lake and from some restaurants in nearby Souk Al Bahar.

The Palace, with Burj Khalifa just behind

Old Town and Souk Al Bahar

Return to The Dubai Mall where you exited the mall, then turn right across the small footbridge to reach 'Old Town Island'. This is part of the extensive **Old Town** development: a swathe of low-rise, sand-coloured buildings with traditional Moorish styling. This area is atmospheric, particularly when lit up at night, with paved areas for pedestrians to walk along, making it one of the easier places to explore on foot.

On the far side of the footbridge lies **Souk Al Bahar** ⑮ ('Souk of the Sailor'; www.soukalbahar.ae; Sat–Thu 10am–10pm, Fri 2–10pm), a small, Arabian-themed mall with 100 stores including a small selection selling traditional handicrafts and a few independent fashion outlets. Restaurants line the waterfront terrace outside, offering views of the Burj Khalifa and Dubai Fountain after dark (timings vary).

On the far side of the Souk Al Bahar stands the opulent **The Palace – The Old Town** ⑯ (see page 105), its sumptuous Moorish-style façade and richly decorated interior offering a surreal contrast to the futuristic needle of the Burj Khalifa rising directly behind it. For food, the hotel's stylish **Thiptara** restaurant, see ③, offers a memorable venue for an upmarket evening meal.

Food and drink

① THE NOODLE HOUSE

Boulevard at Emirates Towers; tel: 800 666 353, www.jumeirah.com; Sun–Thu noon–midnight, Fri–Sat 1pm– midnight; $$
Something of a local institution, this cheerful noodle bar (with venues around town) has a good selection of reasonably priced Thai, Chinese, Malay, Singaporean, Indonesian and Japanese dishes served up at long communal tables. Reservations aren't accepted, so you may have to queue during busy periods.

② SHAKESPEARE & CO.

Al Saqr Business Tower, Sheikh Zayed Road; tel: 04 331 1757; www.shakespeare-and-co. com; daily 17am–midnight; $$
A chintzy European-style café tucked away halfway down Sheikh Zayed Road and a nice place for a coffee or light lunch. The menu includes soups, salads, sandwiches and crepes along with substantial mains.

③ THIPTARA

The Palace Hotel Downtown Dubai; tel: 04 888 3444; www.theaddress.com; daily 6–11.30pm; $$$$
If you fancy pushing the boat out in Downtown Dubai, this beautiful Thai restaurant is the place to head for. Set in a traditional wooden pavilion jutting out into the waters of the lake behind the Dubai Mall, it offers amazing views of the Burj Khalifa and Dubai Fountain. The menu concentrates on sumptuous Bangkok-style seafood, plus meat and a few veg options.

Jumeirah Mosque's dome interior

JUMEIRA AND UMM SUQEIM

This day–long route starts with a visit to the Jumeira Mosque and offers many attractions in the affluent expat suburban strip close to the beach, before heading south to the spectacular Burj Al Arab and Madinat Jumeira – two of modern Dubai's most memorable attractions.

DISTANCE: 14km (8.7 miles)
TIME: A full day
START: Jumeira Mosque
END: Madinat Jumeira
POINTS TO NOTE: Take a taxi to reach the starting point of the route at Jumeira Mosque; you'll also need to catch cabs for short hops down the coastal road at various points; none should cost more than around Dhs10–15. As part of the plans for the area, when the Dubai Canal opens (possibly as early as 2017), Jumeira Road may be changed to one way traffic (heading south-to-north, towards the city). If you find the roads have changed when you visit, start the day at Jumeira Mosque (you can also walk to Jumeira Open Beach or the surrounding cafés), then take a taxi along to Kite Beach and reverse the route via Majlis Ghorfat Um Al Sheif and Mercato, to Mercato mall, where you can take another taxi back to Jumeirah Beach Hotel, and walk the rest of the way to the Madinat Jumeirah.

One of Dubai's wealthiest residential areas, **Jumeira** was traditionally home to many rich expatriate residents and their tanned and manicured wives (popularly, if rather disparagingly, known as 'Jumeira Janes'). With the growth of Dubai, the focus for expats has shifted somewhat to areas further from the city centre due to the plethora of new developments, but the area is always developing, offering a great deal to see and do for visitors. Most of the Jumeira area is decidedly suburban, although there are a number of attractions, including assorted beaches, malls, hotels, restaurants and cafés, while the neighbouring district of Umm Suqeim is home to a cluster of landmark attractions, including the iconic Burj Al Arab hotel.

Jumeira Mosque

The route begins at the striking **Jumeira Mosque ❶**. This is one of the most attractive mosques in Dubai, and also the only one that non-Muslims can visit, via tours run by the **Sheikh Mohammed Centre for Cultural**

Mercato shopping mall

Understanding (www.cultures.ae; tours Sat–Thu 10am). Tours begin with entertaining and informative talks by a local Emirati guide after which the floor is thrown open to questions. There's no need to book, but you should be at the mosque 15 minutes before the tour starts (conservative clothing is a must). For a drink or early lunch after your tour, head for either **Japengo Café**, see ❶, or **Lime Tree Café**, see ❷, both within a stone's throw of the mosque.

Jumeira Road

From the mosque, the seafront Jumeira Road (aka Beach Road) runs straight down the coast all the way to the end of the route at the Madinat Jumeirah. The section of road immediately south of the mosque is lined with a series of small and rather old-fashioned malls with little of attraction to tourists.

Heading down any of the side roads on the west side of Jumeira Road brings you to **Jumeira Public Beach** ❷ – a spacious expanse of free sandy beach, which has some basic facilities, but is less attractive than Jumeira Beach Park further down the road, and not quite as hip as Kite Beach. A new corniche runs down beside the beach all the way through Jumeira (from the Dubai Marine Beach Resort) to the Burj Al Arab, with a walkway, a jogging track and a cycle path.

If you are after a treat, **Nikki Beach Dubai** (www.nikkibeach.com/destinations/beach-clubs/dubai) is a day resort on the Pearl Jumeirah which offers a sublime beach and pool destination (for over 21s only) in which to to relax and spoil yourself.

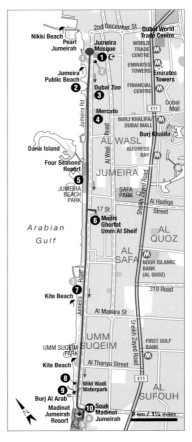

In Safa Park

It's about 1km (0.6 mile) down Jumeira Road from the mosque to the Dubai Zoo; a rather boring walk, and worth avoiding by catching a cab (Dhs10). Alternatively, you may decide to skip the zoo altogether and head straight for the Mercato mall.

Dubai Zoo
Founded in 1967, the **Dubai Zoo** ❸ (www.dm.gov.ae; daily except Tue, 10am–6pm) is the oldest zoo on the Arabian peninsula, although it's very much looking its age, with overcrowded pens housing a motley assortment of random animals including giraffes, tigers, lions, chimps and brown bears, as well as local species including Arabian wolves and oryx. Current conditions for the animals are less than ideal, and there are plans underway to move to a new Safari park-type location, although this has been talked about since 2009.

Mercato
The largest of the various malls lining Jumeira Road, the quirky **Mercato** ❹ (www.mercatoshoppingmall.com; daily 10am–10pm) is well worth a look for its kitsch but entertaining décor. The whole place is designed to resemble a miniature Italian city, with a long central atrium lined by a balconied palazzi and side-alleys heading off to a pair of intimate plazas on either side – a nice spot for a quiet coffee. There's a good selection of upmarket boutiques too, aimed squarely at the wealthy local expat set.

Jumeira Beach Park
Around 3km (1.8 miles) south of Mercato, **Jumeira Beach Park** was the most attractive public beach in the city, with a shady green park leading right up to the beach, and well worth the modest admission fee. Unfortunately, it was razed to make way for the exit of the Dubai Canal out to sea, and is in the process of being rebuilt. Current estimates put it as reopening in mid-late 2017, so keep your eyes peeled if you're in Dubai then, and check the Dubai Municipality website (www.dm.gov.ae) for full details when it's open again.

Safa Park & Dubai Canal
Safa Park (main entrance on Al Wasl Road; www.dm.gov.ae) previously provided Dubai's biggest expanse of greenery, but has since shrunk with the routing of the Dubai Canal through the park, cutting the area by nearly half. However, the park is still a popular place for Dubai's residents to visit, with many attractions and open spaces, and the area will see further development when the canal is finally completed, sometime in 2017. Extending Dubai Creek by 3km (1.8 miles) and cutting back through to the sea from Business Bay, the **Dubai Canal** will be lined with walkways, restaurants and a shopping mall with a

Majlis Ghorfat Umm Al Sheif

park on its rooftop, with hotels and new housing developments closeby, before heading out to sea by a marina and the revamped Jumeira Beach Park.

Majlis Ghorfat Umm Al Sheif

Continuing south along the coastal Jumeira Road for another 2km (1.2 miles) until you reach 17 Street on your left, where a large brown sign points to the venerable old **Majlis Ghorfat Umm Al Sheif** 6 (www.dubaiculture.gov.ae/en; Sun–Thu 7.30am–2.30pm, closed Fri & Sat), 100m down the road on your left. Originally constructed in 1955, the two-storey *majlis* (meeting room) offers a touching throwback to earlier and simpler times, with its traditional coral-stone-walls, shady verandas and teak doors. The *majlis* was originally the summer resort for Dubai's former ruler Sheikh Rashid, serving as the venue for many meetings where the sheikh plotted Dubai's transformation from Arabian backwater to international super-city.

UMM SUQEIM

South of the Majlis Ghorfat Um Al Sheif you enter the suburb of **Umm Suqeim** (although the entire area is usually, if inaccurately, referred to as Jumeira), which is home to three of Dubai's most famous modern landmarks.

About five minutes from the Jumeira Beach Park area (8km from Mercato), located just off Jumeira Road south of Dubai Offshore Sailing Club (DOSC), **Kite Beach** 7 is a free beach that is very popular with Dubai residents for swimming, as well as surfing and kite surfing when the wind and waves allow. Next to the beach is a growing collection of **restaurants and cafés**, see 3, offering a good mix of types of cuisine, along with ice cream, fruit juices and smoothies – all perfect for lunch or snacking to keep your energy levels up.

Just next door is the largest skatepark in the Middle East, **XDubai skatepark** (www.xdubai.com/skatepark), and the **Wire World adventure park** (www.wireworldparks.com). If you end up hot and looking for shade and greenery, Dubai's newest park, **The Journey**, is now open just inland from the beach, and is an especially great place for kids to play.

Jumeirah Beach Hotel

Opened in 1997, the vast **Jumeirah Beach Hotel** 8 (or 'JBH' as it's often known) was the first of the city's mega-hotels, a 100m- (328ft-) high colossus built in the form of a gigantic breaking wave (although from some angles it looks more like a kind of rollercoaster). The hotel has been overtaken by even more exclusive and upmarket hotels elsewhere in the city, but it remains one of southern

Wild Wadi Water Park   *The Burj Al Arab by night*

Dubai's most distinctive and engaging landmarks.

Wild Wadi Water Park

Immediately behind the hotel lies the perennially popular **Wild Wadi Water Park** (www.jumeirah.com; daily Nov–Feb 10am–6pm, Mar–Oct 10am–7pm, but Thu 10am–6pm). This superb, state-of-the-art water park boasts a huge range of watery thrills and spills, ranging from lazy rivers and wave pools for younger kids through to water slides and power jets, plus the stomach-churning 'Jumeirah Sceirah' that drops you 33m (108ft) at speeds of up to 80kph (50mph).

BURJ AL ARAB

Towering over the coastline just beyond the JBH is the stupendous **Burj Al Arab** ❾ (www.jumeirah.com), opened in 1999. Inspired by the shape of a huge, billowing sail, this marvellous high-rise hotel is one of Dubai's most memorable modern landmarks, its hugely distinctive and instantly recognisable outline providing the city with a defining landmark to rival the Eiffel Tower, Sydney Opera House or Big Ben.

The city's most exclusive hotel is popularly dubbed the world's first 'seven-star' hotel on account of the super-fuelled levels of luxury provided to guests in the hotels 200-odd suites. Access to the interior is limited to hotel guests or those with a confirmed reservation at one of the hotel's alluring but expensive bars and restaurants, although it's worth the cash to book in for at least afternoon tea or the sundowner cocktail package at the Skyview Bar on the top floor, to catch a glimpse of the remarkable interior with its cavernous, multicoloured atrium, decorated in huge swathes of gold, red and blue.

MADINAT JUMEIRAH

Immediately south of the Burj Al Arab rises the mighty **Madinat Jumeirah complex** ❿ (www.jumeirah.com). The resort is a sight to behold; built in a form of a self-contained faux-Arabian city, its huge sand-coloured buildings topped with innumerable wind towers and criss-crossed with miniature canals.

Centrepiece of the complex is the lovely **Souk Madinat Jumeirah**, a superb mock-Arabian bazaar with winding alleyways lined with upmarket handicraft shops under elaborate wooden roofs and hanging lanterns. At the far end of the souk, a series of terraces tumble down to the canal below, lined with restaurants and bars, including the excellent **Al Makan** restaurant, see ❹, which is ideal for sampling rarely-found Emirati food.

Either side of the souk are the opulent buildings of the complex's

The Madinat Jumeirah complex

two main hotels. To the north, the stunning **Mina A'Salam** is home to, among other venues, the **Bahri Bar**, see ⑤, the perfect place to enjoy stunning views over the resort and out to the Burj Al Arab, especially for pre-dinner drinks during happy hour (Sat, Sun, Mon, Wed, 4–8pm) when you can enjoy half-price cocktails. To the south, the even more opulent **Al Qasr** is well worth a visit for its spectacular foyer, with vast chandeliers, burbling fountains and vast quantities of marble.

Food and drink

① JAPENGO CAFÉ

Palm Strip Shopping Mall, Jumeira Road; tel: 04 345 4579; Fri–Wed 10am–1am, Thu 10am–2am; $$

Chic modern café-restaurant, with a shamelessly eclectic menu featuring everything from sushi and stir fries through to pizzas and lamb chops. You'll also find a good selection of sandwiches and salads. There's another branch overlooking the canal in the Souk Madinat Jumeirah.

② LIME TREE CAFÉ

Near Spinneys, Jumeira Road; tel: 04 349 8498; daily 7.30am–6pm; $$

Set in an attractive modern villa, this neat little café offers a classic slice of expat Jumeira life. Healthy specialities include outstanding carrot cake, tasty wraps and delicious smoothies.

③ KITE BEACH

Kite Beach

Right next to the beach, an eclectic cluster of eateries has sprung up, offering everything from slices of pizza, Mexican fare and wraps to burgers and frozen bananas, at both kiosks and sit-down cafés. Everything you need to stay cool and fuelled for your day at the beach.

④ AL MAKAN

Souk Madinat Jumeirah; tel: 04 368 6593; www.alkoufa.com; daily noon–1am, Thu/Fri until 2am; $$

Al Makan offers a rare chance to sample authentic Emirati cuisine in a restaurant setting, along with a good selection of Lebanese mezze and grills. Outdoor terrace seating overlooks the Burj Al Arab hotel.

⑤ BAHRI BAR

Souk Madinat Jumeirah; tel: 04 432 3232; www.jumeirah.com; Sat–Mon 4pm–2am, Tue–Fri until 3am

One of the most captivating bars in Dubai, with beautiful Moorish décor, artefacts and to-die-for views over the Madinat Jumeirah to the towering Burj Al Arab opposite.

Dubai Marina

DUBAI MARINA AND PALM JUMEIRAH

The southern end of the city is characterised by its modern developments: high-rise Dubai Marina and Palm Jumeirah, the world's largest man-made island.

DISTANCE: 25km (15.5 miles)
TIME: Half-day/full day
START: The Beach, JBR
END: One&Only Mirage, Al Sufouh
POINTS TO NOTE: You could easily spend a full day exploring the places described here – especially if you stay on the beach for long, or if you devote some time to the various in-house attractions at the Atlantis resort, including the Aquaventure waterpark and Dolphin Bay. In terms of transport, you'll need to catch several cabs to get between the places described below, although depending on where you're staying you can possibly save money by catching the metro down to Dubai Marina station at the beginning of the tour, catching a cab from there to the starting point, and then taking the metro back from the same station at the end of the day.

Bounding the southern end of the city is the vast new **Dubai Marina** development (aka Marsa Dubai or 'New Dubai', as it's sometimes called). This entire district is effectively a brand new city-within-the-city: a swathe of densely packed skyscrapers which have mush-roomed out of the desert with magical rapidity over the past 20 years. Even by Dubai standards, the speed and scale of the development here is astonish-ing, especially for those who remem-ber this part of Dubai in its earlier days, when the entire area was all desert, with only a modest line of hotels fringing the coast. For tourists, the heart of the Marina is **The Beach** and **The Walk** – two developments on the western side of the area which have shopping, din-ing and leisure options right on the long expanse of beach, and also, if you're staying here, the string of upmarket beachside hotels lining the coast.

The Beach
The entire area along the beachfront between the Sheraton and Hilton hotels has been developed as **The Beach at Jumeirah Beach Residence ❶** (www.thebeach.ae), or JBR, as it is known, a residential area comprising 40 tow-ers that house around 15,000 people.

Jumeirah Beach Residences

The beach itself is one of the finest in the city, with a good swathe of broad white sand. Leisure options at The Beach include the Reel Cinema, mini golf, a jogging track, camel rides, the Splash Pad kids' water park, and even free yoga sessions.

The area is also home to **The Market** (www.thebeach.ae; Fri & Sat 10am–10pm, although they do change in the summer), which has a wide selection of stalls set up along the promenade, selling clothes, jewellery and other collectables by local and expat craftsmen, designers and artists; locally grown produce; and other food and drink.

Most of the rest of this strip has been colonized by various hotels, and nearly all have watersports centres (apart from the Ritz-Carlton), that offer various activities including sailing, windsurfing, kayaking, wakeboarding, water-skiing and parasailing. It's also possible to use the beaches, pools and other facilities at many of the hotels for a (usually rather steep) fee.

The Walk

Also in JBR, an attractive pedestrianised promenade known as **The Walk ②** (http://thewalk.ae) runs along the back

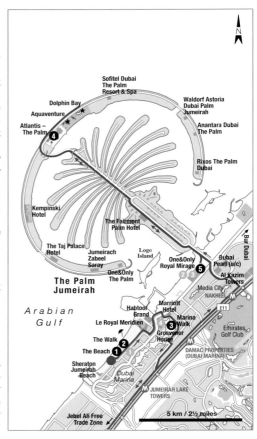

The Walk   *The manmade shape of Palm Jumeirah*

of the beach, and is home to dozens of cafés and restaurants; and a large selection of shops including the popular high-end department store, Boutique 1. **Zaatar W Zeit**, see ①, serves up fast food with a Lebanese twist, and is a good lunch option.

Marina Walk

From here, you can either take a stroll to the north end of the beach, turning inland past Le Royal Meridien and Habtoor Grand hotels, then (carefully) cross the main road and go down the side of the Dubai Marriott Harbour Hotel, or alternatively walk straight to the Marina and head for the **Marina Walk** ❸, an impressive and expansive pedestrian promenade which runs around the edge of the Dubai Marina, lined with a long string of further cafés and restaurants. The Marina itself is a man-made sea inlet, around 1.5km (0.9 mile) long, dotted with luxury yachts and hemmed in by a positive forest of skyscrapers. It's an impressive sight, although the haphazard layout of the entire area, with random high-rises crammed pell-mell into every available space, serves as a chastening memorial to the super-fuelled property boom of the mid-noughties –from whose after-effects the city is still recovering.

PALM JUMEIRAH

From the Marina, hop in a cab for the ride across to Atlantis at the far end of **Palm Jumeirah**. Billed as the 'Eighth Wonder of the World', this vast artificial island first opened in 2006, and is currently the world's largest man-made island, doubling the length of the Dubai coastline at a cost of around $12 billion.

Designed in the form of a palm tree, the drive onto the island, along the main road, runs down the central 'trunk' of the tree (adding a whole new dimension to the expression 'trunk road'), and 16 fronds (each guarded by a security checkpoint) fan out either side, lined with luxury villas, each with their own little slice of private beach at the end of their gardens.

Work is still progressing on the string of resort hotels which will eventually line the outermost stretch of the island, but new venues are opening all the time and currently include One&Only The Palm, Jumeirah Zabeel Saray, Kempinski Hotel & Residences, Sofitel Dubai The Palm Resort & Spa, Waldorf Astoria and Rixos The Palm Dubai (see page 105).

Unfortunately, you can only really appreciate the unique layout of the island from the air; from the ground, the whole thing looks like suburban clutter, while the architecture along the main trunk road is decidedly humdrum, at least until you approach the far end of the island, when the grandiose Atlantis The Palm resort looms ahead.

Atlantis The Palm

At the far end of the Palm, the large façade of **Atlantis The Palm** ❹ (www.atlantisthepalm.com) rears into view above the seafront. The resort is an almost identikit

In Atlantis Hotel's Lost Chambers

copy of its sister establishment, the Atlantis Paradise Island resort in the Bahamas, with the addition of the few discrete Islamic touches, looking like some enormous Disney palace, although despite the sheer size of the place, it lacks the quirky charm and opulent detailing of other modern developments in the city.

Inside, the hotel is unabashedly over-the-top. Entering the main foyer, you're confronted by Dale Chihuly's extraordinary installation in the lobby – a towering glass sculpture looking like a huge waterfall of blue, green, pink and orange noodles. From here, corridors stretch away in either direction, lined with fat gold columns and vast chandeliers.

Atlantis attractions

Atlantis boasts a host of (expensive) in-house attractions. Inside the hotel itself, the kooky **Lost Chambers** (daily 10am–11pm; Dhs100; children under 12, Dhs70) seems to consist of the remains of the legendary city of Atlantis itself, featuring a sequence of underwater halls and tunnels, dotted with specially constructed 'ruins'. This is Dubai at its most shamelessly cheesy, although you may enjoy the sheer absurdity of the idea, and the view of approximately 65,000 resident fish swimming around the submerged faux-classical remains.

In the grounds you'll find the resort's **Aquaventure** waterpark (charge, free to in-house guests), home to a pulse-quickening selection of water coasters, slides and power jets, plus the massive Ziggurat which holds the nail-biting Leap of Faith waterslide, dropping those brave enough to tackle it down into a plastic tunnel in the middle of a lagoon full of sharks. There are also gentler activities for kids, while visitors can also use the fine stretch of private beach next door.

Next door, **Dolphin Bay** offers the chance to swim with the hotel's troupe of resident bottlenose dolphins. Shallow-water interactions cost Dhs850,

---

Artificial islands

Palm Jumeirah has already added 68km (42 miles) to the emirate's coastline, although this is just the first of four proposed offshore developments, intended to create up to 500km (310 miles) of new waterfront. Two further palm-shaped islands are already in the pipeline: the Palm Jebel Ali, 20km (12 miles) further down the coast, and the gargantuan Palm Deira, right next to the city centre. Both are currently stalled due to financial difficulties, although large-scale reclamation works have already been finished. Even more fanciful is the extravagant The World development, a vast complex of artificial islands constructed in the approximate shape of a map of the world, with many of the world's countries represented by their own islands (larger countries have been subdivided into several islands), but as with many mega projects in Dubai, development of the islands has halted in the wake of the global financial crisis

The One&Only Royal Mirage

deep-water interactions (over 12s only) Dhs1025, plus there are observer passes (Dhs300; only available to visitors accompanying those taking part in full interactions). The hefty price tag also includes same-day admission to Aquaventure and the private beach.

Eating on the Palm

There are a number of upmarket restaurants in the hotels on the Palm, including several in Atlantis, though it's worth returning to the mainland after (or just before) dark to sample some of the nightlife in the Marina or the area around it, which boasts a slew of excellent, and generally much more affordable (though still not exactly cheap), places to eat and drink. One superb place to head for is the majestic **One&Only Royal Mirage** ⑤, a captivating, Moorish-style resort which sprawls down the coast for the best part of a kilometre, wrapped in thousands of palm-trees and particularly impressive after dark. Restaurants here include the innovative **Nina's**, see ②, and **Tagine**, see ③. Alternatively, head for the chic **Grosvenor House Hotel**, home to a further collection of alluring places to eat and drink, including **Buddha Bar**, see ④.

Food and drink

① ZAATAR W ZEIT

The Walk, JBR; 04 423 3778; daily 10am–midnight; $

Cheery Lebanese-style fast food, with salads, wraps and pizzas alongside various kinds of *manakish* (a kind of Middle Eastern-style pizza) and other Lebanese-style snacks.

② NINA'S

Arabian Courtyard, One&Only Royal Mirage; tel: 04 399 9999; www.oneandonlyresorts.com; Mon–Sat 7–11.30pm
$$$$

Innovative modern Indian restaurant, combining subcontinental flavours with international ingredients and cooking techniques – anything from traditional butter chicken through to frogs' legs and rambutan.

③ TAGINE

The Palace, One&Only Royal Mirage tel: 04 399 9999; www.oneandonlyresorts.com; Tue–Sun 7pm–1am; $$$$

This exquisitely decorated little Moroccan restaurant is one of the most appealing in the city, with Arabian Nights décor and a fine range of traditional Moroccan cuisine, including a delicious selection of tagines, spicy *harira* (soup), lamb's brain and pigeon pie.

④ BUDDHA BAR

Grosvenor House, Dubai Marina; tel: 04 317 6000; www.buddhabar-dubai.com; daily 7.30pm–2am, Thu/Fri until 3am; $$$$

One of Dubai's most impressive restaurants, this swanky eatery (and bar) is modelled after its famous Parisian namesake, and offers a fine selection of Japanese, Thai and Chinese dishes.

An abra on Dubai Creek

CREEK CRUISES

For a magical way to view Dubai, step on board a traditional dhow or abra and enjoy a breezy ride on the waters of Dubai Creek with optimum views of the old city centre.

TIME: 1–2 hours
START/END: Dubai Creek
POINTS TO NOTE: Take a taxi from your hotel to the starting point for your dhow cruise on Dubai Creek (operators are based in various locations). Companies such as Tour Dubai (tel: 04 336 8407; www.tour-dubai.com) can pick you up from your hotel. It is best to book your dhow cruise at least one day in advance to avoid disappointment.

One of the best ways of exploring Dubai Creek is either by chartering your own *abra* or by going on a dinner cruise aboard one of the dozens of traditional wooden *dhows* which ply the waters after dark. This is a memorable way to enjoy the old city, with marvellous views of the surrounding creekside buildings, including the eclectic tangle of traditional wind-towered buildings and soaring minarets in Bur Dubai, and the futuristic high-rises of Deira.

A cruise also offers a closer look at the dozens of venerable old wooden *dhows* which still motor sedately up and down the Creek, as well as transporting goods further afield to destinations such as Iran and India. The design of the traditional Arabian *dhow is* little changed today from a hundred years past, although modern boats now rely on engine-power rather than oars and sails of yesteryear. The name *dhow* comes from the Swahili word for boat, *dau*.

Abra tours

As well as the short five-minute hop across the Creek by traditional *abra*, it's also possible to charter one of these old-fashioned boats for longer tours up and down the Creek. Chartering an *abra* costs Dhs100 per hour, and the drivers will take you wherever you fancy. An hour's cruise will allow you to ride from the old centres of Bur Dubai or Deira up the creek to the Dubai Creek Golf Club and back again. To find an *abra* for hire, head to the nearest *abra* station and ask around. Note that the rate of Dhs100 per hour is officially fixed (and posted in writing at all *abra* stations) and the same regardless of how many people use the boat, so don't be

Enjoying a dinner cruise

A more modern water taxi

hassled into paying more. Take whatever food and drink you might need with you.

Dhow cruises

A more comfortable alternative to chartering an *abra* is one of the popular evening **dinner cruises** (see page 34) – these can be booked through any of the city's tour operators, while many hotels can also arrange trips. Most cruises are aboard traditional old wooden *dhows*, offering a leisurely overview of the city. Cruises generally last two hours, departing at around 8–8.30pm and cost anything from Dhs150 to Dhs350, inclusive of a buffet dinner.

Independent cruise operators include Rikks Cruises (tel: 04 357 2200; www.rikks.net), which offers some of the cheapest cruises in town, while the more upmarket Al Mansour Dhow is operated by the Radisson Blu hotel (tel: 04 205 7333; www.radissonblu.com). For a more modern alternative, Bateaux Dubai (tel: 04 399 4994; www.jaresortshotels.com) runs cruises in its state-of-the-art glass-sided modern boat, offering a touch more luxury than other operators, plus better-than-average food.

Water taxis

For a more modern way to get around by water than *abra*, you can book an air-conditioned water taxi to shuttle around various points on Dubai Creek, or to take you as far south as The Palm Jumeirah, Dubai Marina and Jebel Ali. Taxis are run by RTA (Roads and Transport Authority; www.rta.

ae), and bookings can be made on their website, by phone, or through your hotel. Prices are not cheap, but travelling with a good number makes it a reasonable value, and it's a great way to see the city from a new and unique angle, especially the offshore developments.

Medieval ships

The daring and prowess of medieval Arab sailors has become the stuff of legend, inspiring legendary tales of Sinbad the Sailor and many other mariners' yarns. At the height of Gulf trade in the 9th century, Gulf seamen were sailing all the way to China, sometimes making massive profits en route, although often experiencing hair-raising shipwrecks and other maritime misadventures en route. Despite the romantic legends, the life of the medieval Arab seaman was a hard one, spending days and nights exposed to the elements, often in conditions of extreme hardship. Crew were expected to accommodate themselves as best they could on top of the cargo, while ablutions were carried out in a precarious box slung out over the side of the boat. Most seafaring boats were surprisingly small, built using the traditional 'sewn' construction, with the planks of boats not nailed but literally stitched together using coconut twine, caulked with a mixture of coir and fish oil, a mode of ship building that came as a surprise to Europeans and Arabs from the Mediterranean, such as Marco Polo and Ibn Battuta.

DESERT AND MOUNTAINS

No visit to Dubai is complete without a foray into the desert, which stretches inland to the south of the city, offering a brief taste of the mighty sands which cover most of the Arabian Peninsula. Further inland, the rugged Hajar Mountains provide a very different landscape to the desert and the coast.

DISTANCE: 250km (155 miles) round trip
TIME: A full day or overnight
START/END: Central Dubai
POINTS TO NOTE: Regular buses run between Dubai and Hatta (www.dubai-buses.com; daily 6am–9pm; hourly from the Gold Souk Bus Station, Deira). But if you want to experience the desert on the way, and explore the surrounding area, you should rent a car (see page 130) or go with an organised tour. Unless you have lots of experience off-road driving in desert conditions, the safest way to see the desert properly is to book a safari with a licensed tour operator. Fridays and public holidays are generally a lot busier, so if you can avoid these times, you'll have a more pleasurable experience. If you want to stay overnight, the Hatta Fort Hotel is recommended, or book an overnight tour which takes in the desert one day, including camping, and the mountains the next.

If you are after a full-on trip into the desert, these are best arranged by sign-ing up for a tour with one of Dubai's many operators – most tours put the emphasis firmly on a stereotypical mish-mash of dune-driving, belly-dancing and other touristy crowd-pleasers, although there are some more rewarding (and peaceful) alternatives available if you shop around. A good time to experience the desert is late in the afternoon, when the light is as soft and warm as the sand underfoot, while after dark the night sky, away from any ambient light, is remarkably clear.

Around 65 per cent of the 85,000 sq km (33,000 sq miles) of the UAE is desert. The term encompasses a variety of landscapes and conditions: as well as rolling dunes, it includes salt flats (*sabkha*), flood plains, mountains and dry valleys (*wadis*). The desert that begins on the outskirts of Dubai (or more accurately within the city limits, where every vacant lot is sandy) forms part of the Saharo-Arabian Desert, the most extensive dry zone in the world, which stretches away into Oman and Saudi Arabia, covering most of the Arabian peninsula. Not surprisingly, the

4x4 desert safari in the dunes

further you get from Dubai, the more unspoilt the scenery becomes – much of the desert in the immediate vicinity of the city has been more or less ruined by huge highways, petrol stations, looming pylons and swathes of random development.

Big Red

The most popular desert destination close to Dubai is the complex by a large dune, commonly known as '**Big Red**' ❶, next to the main highway E44, about halfway between Dubai and Hatta. This huge mountain of sand is impressive at any time of day, but particularly magical towards dusk, when the low light turns it to a rich, russet red. Unfortunately, the dunes' natural majesty are somewhat compromised by the hordes of four-wheel drives and quad bikes, which can be seen at pretty much any time of day struggling up and down the dunes' steep sides, like hyperactive ants. However, it doesn't take too long to drive past it into the desert before you can find your own spot of peace and quiet to enjoy the scenery. The slightly smaller (but still mightily impressive) swathe of dunes on the southern side of the highway is a popular dune-bashing destination for local tour companies.

Dubai Desert Conservation Reserve

For a much more peaceful desert experience, the best place to head is the superb **Dubai Desert Conser-vation Reserve** ❷ (www.ddcr.org), around 45km (28 miles) from Dubai next to the main E66 highway to Al Ain. The reserve encloses 225 sq km of low, shifting dunes, dotted with hardy ghaf trees, and serves as a refuge for over thirty local species of mammal and reptile, including rare creatures such as the oryx, Arabian gazelle, sand gazelle, Arabian red fox and sand fox. Access to the reserve is carefully controlled. The cheapest option is to come on a visit with one of the select group of Dubai tour operators who are allowed to run tours here (including Arabian Adventures: www.arabian-adventures.com). Alternatively, you can stay in the reserve at the idyllic, but spectacularly expensive, **Al Maha Resort** (see page 107).

Where to eat

While there aren't any restaurants mentioned on this route, the 'Big Red' area does have some cafeteria options nearby, or if you're part of an organised tour, all food and drinks will be provided en route (and afternoon safaris typically culminate in a lavish buffet dinner at a desert camp). In the mountains, there are options for eating out, and shops to stock up on food and drinks, but if you're travelling independently, it's best to take whatever food you're likely to need, plus large amounts of water – it's easy to get seriously dehydrated in the desert heat.

Observing wildlife at Dubai Desert Conservation Reserve

Fossil Rock

Another popular desert destination is **Fossil Rock ❸**, part of the craggy Jebel Maleihah – an impressive outcrop of rock standing in splendid isolation amidst the sands and looking a bit like an enormous decaying tooth. The rock is named after the marine-life fossils that can be found in it, proof that these rocks (like many in this part of the UAE and Oman) were formed underwater. The rock lies around 50km (31 miles) from Dubai, just south of the main road (S116) from Sharjah to Khor Kalba and Fujairah. Again, this can be reached by 4x4 (including from Big Red) if you're being driven by a competent desert driver, but you can even get close enough to it by 2WD on hard tracks (from Maleihah village on the E55, Madam–Dhaid road), to allow you to walk up to it across the dunes.

Be prepared

Although generally not as humid as the coast, the desert can, of course, get extremely hot during the day. Make sure you pack plenty of liquid refreshments (ideally water), sun cream, a hat and sunglasses. If you are going to be out after sunset, pack a jumper – without cloud cover to trap the heat of the day, Arabian nights can be surprisingly chilly (in the winter). It is always safest to travel in convoy, so if you are not going out with a tour group, never get out of your depth with the off-road driving, and make sure you don't venture too far off the beaten track with a local expert with you.

From Fossil Rock, head back to the Madam–Dhaid road and head north. After just a couple of kilometres, turn right onto the Sharjah to Kalba road (S116). Keep heading straight (ignore the E84

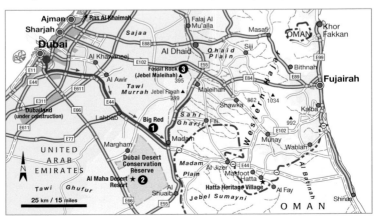

Marine fossils

Fossil Rock and the Jebel Maleihah

to Fujairah), until just before Munay, where there's signs to turn right for Masfoot and Hatta. When you reach the E44 again, turn left to Hatta, or turning right and heading back west will take you past the hilltop summer homes that belong to Dubai's sheikhs and wealthy businessmen and on to some roadside carpet stalls, a popular place to by carpets and pots. For a map of the new route, see the website for the Hatta Fort Hotel (www.jaresortshotels.com).

Until 2015, there were no checkpoints to pass through and the drive took only one hour along the modern Highway 44 through the desert. However, new border rules between the UAE and Oman mean that the small part of Omani land the 44 crossed is now out-of-bounds, so the route to get to Hatta now heads north from Madam, past Fossil Rock, then south east on the E102 and on a picturesque curvy road through the mountains to Hatta. The border post for Oman is actually 10km (6 miles) further to the east of Hatta.

HATTA

Some 110km (68 miles) inland from Dubai, rural **Hatta** ❹ is a small enclave of Dubai territory, surrounded by land belonging to Ajman and Ras Al Khaimah, and neighbouring country Oman. In Hatta itself, when you reach the roundabout with an open-sided fortress in the middle, either turn left for Hatta Fort Hotel, or right for Hatta Heritage Village and the road to the dam.

Desert tours

By far the easiest way to explore the desert is with one of Dubai's numerous specialist tour companies, most of whom offer a range of half-day, full-day and overnight trips (usually with other groups). These tours usually feature some dune-bashing (speeding over the dunes in a four-wheel-drive) and perhaps one or two other activities like sand-skiing or quad-biking, followed by an evening barbecue at a cheesy 'traditional' tented camp with belly-dancer, camel rides, henna-painting and so on. For a more peaceful view of the desert, it's worth spending a night under canvas. A few operators also offer less stereotypical desert trips, perhaps with visits to a local village, date plantation or camel farm.

Dubai's leading operator is Arabian Adventures (tel: 04 303 4888; www.arabian-adventures.com), a professional and well-run outfit offering a wide range of tours, although usually at slightly higher prices than other places. Other reliable operators include Alpha Tours (tel: 04 294 9888, www.alphatoursdubai.com) and Orient Tours (tel: 04 282 8238; www.orienttours.ae). One company which offers more flexible and personalised itineraries for smaller groups, including desert tours with camping, camel trekking, hiking in the mountains and dune buggy rides, is Explorer Tours (04 286 1991; www.explorertours.ae).

A Hatta watchtower

Prehistoric Hatta

The village of Hatta is the only part of the Dubai emirate outside the city, and was traditionally a quiet mountain retreat for residents from Dubai in search of cooler and drier climate during the hot and humid summers. Archaeological finds have revealed that the fertile mountain valleys around Hatta were first inhabited more than 4,000 years ago, during the Bronze Age. Excavations in the Juma valley have uncovered an ancient settlement and tombs similar to those found in Umm Al Nar, Abu Dhabi, dating from c.2,000–2,500BC. Finds from the site are displayed at Dubai Museum (see page 28). There is very little to see in the village, except the Heritage Village and a small hill-top park, but it is nice just to see life here going at a very different pace compared to Dubai.

Heritage Village

Hatta Heritage Village ❺ (tel: 04 852 1374; www.dubaiculture.gov.ae/en; Sat–Thu 7.30am–8.30pm, Fri 2.30–8.30pm; free) brings the community's colourful history to life. Various styles of mountain dwellings have been rebuilt around carefully restored buildings, including the first fort in the emirate of Dubai, constructed in 1790, which now houses a weaponry museum. Check out the fascinating variety of mud and *barasti* (palm frond) houses and a restored *falaj* irrigation system that channels water through the village to the neighbourhood's date-palm gardens. On weekends and public holi-

days, local women in national dress and *burqa* face masks work away at traditional crafts (note that you should always ask their permission before snapping away). The watchtowers that loom high over the village date back to 1850.

Hatta Pools

The heritage village and hotel aside, the main attraction of this area for many were the **Hatta Pools**, which were a short off-road drive south-east of Hatta into the mountains. However, changes in the regulations for the UAE/Oman border have seen all borders closed to any non-local

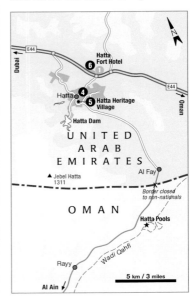

Hatta Pools

(Emirati/Omani) nationals, so for visitors, this route to the pools is now off limits.

If you are determined to visit the pools or just want to access the mountains for hiking, camping etc, it is still possible to drive from Dubai to Al Ain (especially for a multi-day camping trip exploring several routes and locations), pass through both the UAE and Omani border crossings (easiest for those nationalities who can get a visa on arrival), then head north to Mahdah and onto Rayy, and access the pools that way. Detailed route descriptions good enough to get you to classic routes in the mountains (and deserts) of the UAE, can be found in *UAE Off-Road* from Dubai-based Explorer Publishing (http://askexplorer.com/shop/uae-off-road-1912.html), on sale in all bookshops and supermarkets.

Don't expect idyllic pools, cascading waterfalls and a brimming river at Hatta Pools and you won't be disappointed. The stunning but parched landscape around the pools bears comparison with the surface of Mars. The access track is dusty, the river bed largely dry, while the spring pools are made up of low-level, slow-moving water. Throughout the year, there is enough water at crossing points to make a splash in your car though, and there's always enough water for a cooling dip.

Hatta Fort Hotel
The attractive **Hatta Fort Hotel** ❻ (tel: 04 852 3211; www.hattaforthotel.com) is a venerable institution surrounded by dry, jagged, rocky peaks. The complex feels a bit like a safari lodge, with landscaped gardens and fine views over the surrounding mountains. Dubai residents often use the hotel for weekend breaks, with leisure activities such as the swimming pools, archery, mini golf and activities to keep you entertained, even the kids. Even if you are not planning to stay the night, you can lunch at **Gazebo**, see ❶, or for a nominal charge, relax by the pool.

Back to Dubai
To get back to Dubai, retrace your way here through the mountains, picking up route S116 back through the desert, then pick up the E611 then the E44 to take you all the way back into Dubai.

Food and drink

❶ GAZEBO
Hatta Fort Hotel, Hatta; tel: 04 852 3211; www.jaresortshotels.com; daily 7am–8pm; $$–$$$
Located on an air-conditioned balcony above the Hatta Fort Hotel's gorgeous swimming pool, Gazebo offers a marvellous view of the landscaped gardens and the rugged Hajar Mountains beyond, backed up by a well-prepared selection of international dishes. If you're planning on staying overnight, the Jeema restaurant is open for evening meals, and you can enjoy a drink from the Roumoul Cocktail Bar, along with views of the sunset and the stars on the Sunset terrace.

Sharjah's Central Souk

SHARJAH

Just 10km up the coast from Dubai, but light-years distant in terms of attitude and atmosphere, lies the conservative emirate of Sharjah, self-styled 'cultural capital' of the UAE, and home to an interesting range of museums devoted to the region's cultural and Islamic traditions.

DISTANCE: 20km (12 miles)
TIME: A full day
START/END: Dubai
POINTS TO NOTE: The road between Dubai and Sharjah is the most notoriously congested in the UAE, usually descending into total gridlock during the morning and evening rush hours – it's best to travel to Sharjah after 10am, or even later, and return either before 5pm or after 8pm. Buses run 24hr (every 20–30min) from Al Ghubaiba Bus Station in Bur Dubai, dropping you at the bus station in Sharjah about 300m north of Central Souk, and about 750m from the Heritage Area. You might be able to catch a cab, although many drivers are reluctant to go to Sharjah due to the appalling traffic, and fares are subject to a Dhs20 surcharge. Expect the journey to take a minimum of 45min, potentially more than twice that during rush hours.

The UAE's third-largest emirate after Abu Dhabi and Dubai, Sharjah (population 750,000) has a decidedly different flavour from neighbouring Dubai (even though, physically, the two cities are now almost fused in a formless expanse of concrete). Compared to life in free-wheeling, liberal Dubai, Sharjah has clung much more firmly to its traditional cultural roots, exemplified by the fine string of museums which have been set up across the city, as well as by the total ban on alcohol and the more explicit adherence to Sharia-style law – conservative dress and behaviour are advised at all times.

SHARJAH SOUK AND AROUND

At the western end of the city centre, close to the waterfront, stands the vast **Central Market** ❶ (also known as the Blue Souk, Sharjah Souk and Souk Al Markasi). This is the largest souk in the UAE, housed in a striking pair of buildings topped with wind towers and embellished with blue tiles and traditional Islamic designs (although the rounded roof can be likened to a line of oil barrels lying side by side). Inside, the myriad of shops (Sat–Thu 10am–1pm and 4–10pm, closed Fri am) are spread over two levels,

Souq Al Arsa Heritage Area

stuffed with a veritable treasure trove of carpets, antiques and assorted souvenirs. Downstairs is devoted to everyday items including perfumes, cheap shoes and electrical goods, while upstairs has an excellent spread of antique and carpet shops – if you're looking to buy a rug, this is the place to head, although bargaining is, of course, essential. The **Danial** restaurant, see ❶, just behind the souk in the Crystal Plaza, is a good place to stop for food.

Al Mahatta Museum

East of the souk, King Abdul Aziz Street was, until 1976, the main runway of the UAE's first airport, originally established in 1932 as a stopover for flights from London to Australia. The UAE's first hotel, the Fortress, just off King Abdul Aziz Street, has been restored and, with an air-traffic control tower, forms the aviation-themed **Al Mahatta Museum** ❷ (www.sharjahmuseums.ae; Sat–Thu 8am–8pm, Fri 4–8pm), a 10-minute walk from the Central Market. Among the aircraft on display are a World War II-era Avro Anson and a Douglas DC3, which belonged to the Gulf Aviation Co., the forerunner of Gulf Air.

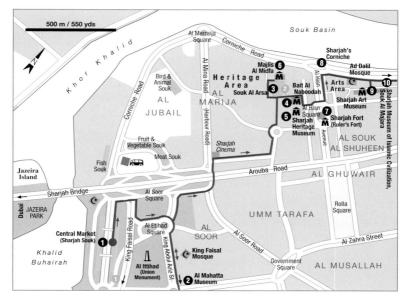

In Sharjah Art Museum

SHARJAH HERITAGE AREA

From Al Mahatta Museum, it's a 20-minute walk or short taxi ride (around Dhs10) to Sharjah's **Heritage Area**. This entire area of traditional houses is being carefully restored as part of the Heart of Sharjah (www.heartofsharjah.ae) – the largest project of its kind in the Middle East, restoring historical buildings and developing the area to promote the city's heritage and culture – and is home to a increasing number of small museums and other attractions, including Souk Al Arsa.

Souk Al Arsa

At the heart of the Heritage Area lies the **Souk Al Arsa ❸** (Sat–Thu 10am–1pm and 4.30–9pm, Fri 4.30–9pm), the UAE's oldest souk, and perhaps its prettiest, with dozens of traditional coral-stone-built shops set around a miniature labyrinth of little alleyways beneath palm-frond roofs. Most of the shops here are devoted to antiques and handicrafts, with an interesting range of mainstream souvenirs and more unusual bric-a-brac for sale. The **Souk Al Arsah Coffee Shop**, see ❷, is a good place for lunch or a drink.

Heritage Area Museums

Several museums stand close to Souk Al Arsa. The interesting **Bait Al Naboodah ❹** (www.sharjahmuseums.ae; Sat–Thu 8am–8pm, Fri 4–8pm) is one of the finest traditional courtyard houses in the UAE, attractively restored with old wooden furniture and assorted artefacts. Renovations were due to be completed in 2016, so it should be back open as usual again by 2017. Opposite the souk and next to **Bait Al Naboodah, Sharjah Heritage Museum ❺** (www.sharjahmuseums.ae; Sat–Thu 8am–8pm, Fri 4–8pm) illustrates the rich heritage and culture of the Emirati people, and shows how the landscapes of the UAE and Arabic traditions have shaped the people to who they are today.

Close by, the diminutive **Majlis Al Midfa ❻** (www.sharjahmuseums.ae; Sat–Thu 8am–8pm, Fri 4–8pm; free) is best known for its much-photographed round wind tower, the only one of its kind in the UAE. The house was formerly home of **Ibrahim bin Mohammed Al Midfa**, founder of the region's first newspaper in 1927 and is now a tiny museum showcasing his personal effects. Another site that started renovations in 2016, it should be up and running by 2017, but check the website for further details.

Sharjah Fort

Heading down any of the narrow streets running east from the Heritage Area brings you to the wide Al Hisn Avenue, running from Rolla Square to the corniche. Plum in the middle of the dual-carriageway avenue sits **Sharjah Fort ❼** (aka Al Hisn Fort or the Ruler's Fort) (www.sharjahmuseums.ae; Tue–Thu, Sat–Sun 9am–1pm and 4–8pm, Fri 4–8pm). The imposing old structure,

Discover Islamic Civilization   *The mosque and buildings along the Corniche*

which formerly served as the residence of the ruling Al Qasimi family, is home to an interesting museum focusing on the history of the city. After significant work, it reopened in 2015, with an enhanced experience for visitors, offering more in-depth exhibits and displays.

ALONG THE CORNICHE

Continue along Al Hisn Avenue to reach **Sharjah's Corniche** ❽. Like the waterfront in Deira (Dubai), this is an impromptu harbour, usually with dozens of traditional wooden *dhows* moored up, and piles of merchandise cluttering the pavement – a fine sight.

Sharjah Art Museum
Turn right along Corniche Street and walk for five minutes, past the modern Iranian Souk, then turn right, away from the water, following the signs to the imposing **Sharjah Art Museum** ❾ (www.sharjah museums.ae; Sat–Thu 8am–8pm, Fri 4–8pm; free). The main attraction here is the permanent collection upstairs, devoted to a fine collection from leading Arabic artists and sculptors. The ground floor of the museum is devoted to temporary exhibitions, usually featuring local Emirati and other Arab artists.

Sharjah Museum of Islamic Civilization
One of city's highlights is the world-class **Sharjah Museum of Islamic Civilization** ❿ (www.sharjahmuseums.ae; Sat–

Thu 8am–8pm, Fri 4–8pm), a further five minutes' walk along the Corniche in the beautifully restored Souk Al Majara, topped with its distinctive golden dome. The museum offers a wide-ranging and excellently presented overview of the contributions made by Muslim scientists, artists and architects to world knowledge over the past 500 years, including absorbing displays on medieval Islamic chemistry, medicine, astronomy and navigation. There are also galleries showcasing Islamic arts and crafts, including ceramics, glass, armour, woodwork, textiles and jewellery.

Food and drink

❶ DANIAL
3rd Floor, Crystal Plaza; 06 574 4668; www.danialrestaurant.com; daily 12.30pm–1.30am; $$
Given the lack of places to eat in Sharjah Souk, this place (in the Crystal Plaza, immediately to the south) is a handy option, with reasonable buffet lunches and a selection of Middle Eastern and Iranian dishes.

❷ SOUK AL ARSAH COFFEE SHOP
Souk Al Arsa, Sharjah Heritage Area; daily 8am–10pm; $
Cute little café in the pretty courtyard at the heart of the Souk Al Arsa – a good place to grab a drink or try one of the café's spicy chicken, mutton or fish biryanis.

A camel on beach in Ajman

THE NORTHERN EMIRATES

The drive from Dubai through the northern emirates is like a journey back in time: the smaller cities of Ajman and Umm Al Quwain offer a view of how Dubai looked before the oil boom, while even the relatively more developed Ras Al Khaimah still has a small town feel compared to Dubai and Sharjah.

DISTANCE: 162km (100 miles) round trip
TIME: A full day
START/END: Dubai
POINTS TO NOTE: A rental car (see page 130) is required for this route. A good plan is to drive north following the coastal road through Sharjah, Ajman and Umm Al Quwain, and then return along the faster, but much less scenic Emirates Road (E311) inland. Whichever way you drive it's a long day-trip if you want to get all the way to Ras Al Khaimah – an early start is recommended. If you don't want to drive, some tour operators in Dubai run tours of Ajman and Ras Al Khaimah, covering most of the sights described below.

The northern emirates extend to Ras Al Khaimah, some 140km (87 miles) from Dubai. As you head north-east, away from Dubai, you pass through notably less-wealthy, less-populous and less-developed parts of the UAE.

To Ajman

From Dubai, drive to Sharjah, aiming for Rolla Square and then turn left down Al Hisn Avenue to reach the seafront corniche. From here, follow the Corniche Road, passing the large Radisson Blu Resort on your left, along a regal avenue of palm trees, wrought-iron railings and a showcase fountain signalling the presence of the Ruler's Palace, also on your left. While it might be tempting to dip into Sharjah's attractions, there's more than enough to keep you busy for a full day in the city, so it's best just to take in the sights and save them for another day (see page 74).

Continue along the coast road into the emirate of Ajman. This is a particularly attractive drive, with a long white-sand beach flanking the road on your left – a bit like a less developed version of Dubai's Jumeira coastline.

AJMAN

Some 10km (6 miles) beyond Sharjah, a modest cluster of high-rises announces the arrival of Ajman itself. In terms of

Ajman Museum

ambience, **Ajman ❶** is much like the Dubai of the 1980s. The smallest of the UAE's seven emirates (250 sq km, 97 sq miles; population 275,000), Ajman has no oil wealth and continues to rely on traditional industries such as boat building and fishing.

Ajman Museum

The main attraction here is the excellent **Ajman Museum** (www.ajmantourism.ae; Sat–Thu 8am–8, closed Fri) in the town's old fort. To reach the museum, take a right turn at the Ajman Beach Hotel and follow the road alongside the edge of the pretty marina to Leewara Street. Turn right and, at the first roundabout, bear left towards Clocktower roundabout and Central Square. The fort will be to your left.

Built in 1775, the fort was the ruler's official residence until 1970, and the museum showcases life in the region from ancient times to the modern era. More appealing in some ways than its Dubai equivalent (the quieter, more parochial setting helps), it boasts a fine wind tower, which, unlike those in some other UAE museums, is fully functioning.

For a good stopping point in Ajman, try **Café Kranzler**, see ❶, in the Kempinski Hotel Ajman among the collection of upmarket beach hotels on the coast.

UMM AL QUWAIN

Continue through Ajman along Hamid Bin Abdul Aziz Street. At the first roundabout head for Al Ittihad Street at 11 o'clock. Carry on until this street joins Badr Street and turn left. You are now on the road to Umm Al Quwain. (If in doubt, follow signs for RAK.) Follow this road for 26km (16 miles), at which point a sign points left to the side road to **Umm Al Quwain ❷**, a further 9km (5.5 miles) distant. After another 5km (3 miles) or so, you reach Umm Al Quwain new town – little more than a rather bedraggled line of low-key shops flanking the main road. The whole place can be spookily quiet during the day.

Umm Al Quwain fishermen

The Old Town

On the far side of the modern town lies **Umm Al Quwain Old Town**, situated on its own sandy headland at the very end of the road. Three ancient watchtowers, once part of a fortified defensive wall, mark the boundary of the old town at the narrowest part of the headland, where King Faisal Road meets Al Soor Street. At this point you will see the old town away to your right across an enormous lagoon. On part of the lagoon's shoreline you will find one of Umm Al Quwain's most appealing attractions – a forest of mangrove trees.

Take the first right and follow the road past a small public park. The town's old fortress stands in a small square beyond the roundabout ahead. This is now open to the public as the **Umm Al Quwain Museum** Ⓐ (Sat–Sun, Tue–Thu 8am–1pm and 5–8pm, Fri 5–8pm).

The restored fort itself offers a welcome contrast to the dusty streets outside, with its pretty coral stone buildings and a neat courtyard. The museum is less appealing, with a dusty collection of artefacts and some unexciting archaeological finds from the nearby site of Ad-Dour.

Boat trips from Flamingo Beach Resort

Take a right at the roundabout and follow Corniche Road past the fish market, where you are likely to see fishermen mending broken nets. Just before the road arcs left to continue its loop through the old town (before rejoining King Faisal Road), turn right into the low-key **Flamingo Beach Resort** (tel: 06 765 0000; http://flamingo.binmajid.com).

The resort offers various activities including boat trips, crab hunting and deep-sea fishing expeditions (advance reservations essential). Boat trips (around

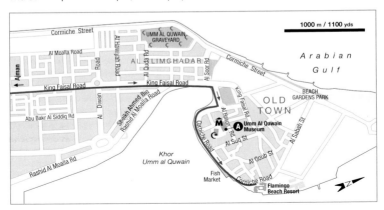

Fort, Umm Al Quwain   *Dreamland Aqua Park*

Dhs200/hour) offer a nice way to see **As Siniyyah ❸** and the various other islands which dot the coast – the habitat of herons, cormorants, flamingos, turtles and even *dugong* (manatees or sea cows). There are plans to develop the island with several eco-style hotels from 2019, plus housing, a marina and a golf course – which may well affect the local wildlife.

Ad-Dour Archaeological Site
Return to your car and retrace your steps back to the main Ras Al Khaimah highway, continuing north for 8km (5 miles) to reach the low stone ruins of **Ad-Dour ❹**, an archaeological site to the right of the highway, opposite Khor Al Beidah. The largest pre-Islamic site on the Arabian Gulf, Ad-Dour (meaning 'the houses' in Arabic) was a major trading centre from around 300BC to AD100 and is a candidate for the great city of Omana, the Dubai of its day, which was known to classical geographers including Strabo and Pliny the Elder.

Dreamland Aqua Park
About 10km (6 miles) further along the highway a sign points off on the left to the **Dreamland Aqua Park ❺** (www.dreamlanduae.com; daily Nov–Feb 10am-6pm, Mar–May & Sep–Oct Fri until 7pm, Jun–Aug weekends until 8pm; Ramadan 10am–4pm; NB: Fri, Sat & holidays strictly family days), an unexpectedly large and well-equipped water park in this rather out-of-the-way location. It is not as state-of-the-art as Wild Wadi and Aqua-

venture in Dubai, but a fair bit cheaper and, during the week, a lot quieter as well. The park has a huge wave pool, family raft rides and twister slides, and overnight camping stays are possible on site, with all equipment provided.

RAS AL KHAIMAH

As soon as you enter the emirate of Ras Al Khaimah, there's a noticeable upturn in development and ambition. Perhaps taking a leaf out of Dubai's success story, the first project lies offshore in the shape of **Al Marjan ❻**, four reclaimed islands that are already home to DoubleTree by Hilton Resort (http://doubletree3.hilton.com) and Marjan Island Resort & Spa (www.accorhotels.com), with many more hotels and residential areas planned.

A little further up the road, past the old local favourite, the Bin Majid, is the developing area of **Al Jazirat Al Hamra ❼** with the impressive Hilton Al Hamra Beach & Golf Resort (www3.hilton.com). Originally known as **Al Hamra Fort Resort**, it was designed in the form of a traditional Arabian fortress and occupies a prime slice of beachfront real estate. The resort is a good option for lunch, with a range of eating venues including **Le Chalet**, see ❷. On the way into town, you'll pass the **Iceland Water Park ❽** (www.icelandwaterpark.com), a superb themed park with masses of rides, well worth stopping by, even compared to Dubai's parks – and it's cheaper; and **The Cove Rotana ❾** (www.rotana.com), a peaceful and spa-

Dhow at sunset, Ras Al Khaimah

cious resort with hotel rooms and villas clustered down a hillside looking out over the sea, offering different atmosphere to the usual beach resort.

Entering the city of **Ras Al Khaimah** ❿ (usually abbreviated to 'RAK'), you'll see the attractive backdrop of the distant redrock mountains of the Musandam Peninsula heading further north in Oman. RAK is notably more built up and livelier than either Ajman or Umm Al Quwain. The central souk area around the fort is worth a look for its traditional street life, busy with robed Emiratis and their wives, veiled from head to toe in black *abayas* – some still wear the traditional Bedu face masks.

Ras Al Khaimah National Museum

The town's fort, once again, has been converted into the **Ras Al Khaimah National Museum** (www.rakheritage. rak.ae; daily 9am–6pm, Fri 3–7.30pm), a rather grand name for a decidedly modest museum that showcases the usual array of local artefacts. The 19th-century fort itself is the main attraction, with a fine wind tower looming over the shady courtyard within. For food, head to **Al Bahar**, see ❸, at the Hilton Ras Al Khaimah Resort & Spa in the north of the city. If you decide to stay over in RAK, you can take a drive up to Jebel Jais – the UAE's highest mountain – for views of the mountains or to hike, explore heritage sites, visit a desert resort or camp, learn about falconry or pamper yourself at a spa (see www.rasalkhaimahtourism.com).

For the return journey to Dubai, you can retrace the way you came, but for a faster, less congested route (if you hit rush hour) take Emirates Road (E311), which bypasses much of the coastal cities, although this can also be busy. Allow an hour or two for your return journey.

Food and drink

① CAFÉ KRANZLER

Kempinski Hotel Ajman; tel: 06 714 5555; www.kempinski.com; daily 7am–10.30pm; $$$

This terrace café-restaurant overlooking the gardens at the upmarket Kempinski is nice for coffee or an early lunch, with tasty international fare including Asian, Middle Eastern and European dishes.

② LE CHALET

Hilton Al Hamra Beach & Golf Resort, Al Jazirat Al Hamra; tel: 07 244 6666; www3.hilton.com; daily 9am–6pm; $$$

Attractive beachfront restaurant overlooking the swimming pool terrace, offering well-prepared light meals, salads and seasonal specials.

③ AL BAHAR

Hilton Ras Al Khaimah Resort & Spa, on the northern side of RAK City; tel: 07 228 8844; www3.hilton.com; daily 12.30am–4pm, 6pm–11pm; $$$

Laidback beachside restaurant serving up tasty Arabic food including a range of mezze and grilled meat and fish.

Al Ain oasis palm trees

AL AIN

The attractive city of Al Ain – the UAE's largest inland settlement, often called The Garden City of the UAE – offers a rewarding day-trip from Dubai, with a cluster of absorbing forts and souks, and one of the country's most beautiful oases.

DISTANCE: 270km
TIME: A full day
START/END: Dubai
POINTS TO NOTE: A car is essential to cover all of the sights in this itinerary, although the first section of the route is eminently walkable, and gives a good taste of the city. If you don't want to drive, regular buses to Al Ain depart from Al Ghubaiba Bus Station in Bur Dubai (1hr 30min; Dhs20). Alternatively, many local tour operators run day trips covering many of the sights listed. The city and surrounding area have more than enough to explore for a two-day trip here.

Al Ain National Museum and The Eastern Fort

Al Ain National Museum ❶ (www.abu dhabi.ae; Sat–Thu 8.30am–7.30pm, Fri 3–7.30pm, closed Mon) is a good starting point for tours of the city, with displays covering local life and artefacts ranging from old Korans and antique silver jewellery through to photos of Abu Dhabi in the 1960s. The **Eastern Fort** (aka Sul-

tan Fort; www.abudhabi.ae; Sat–Thu 8.30am–7.30pm, Fri 3–7.30pm; free), is located right next to the museum, and is one of 20-odd forts in Al Ain and the surrounding desert. It's best known as the birthplace of Sheikh Zayed Bin Sultan Al Nahyan, ruler of Abu Dhabi and the first President of the UAE, who oversaw the emirate's transformation from backwater Arabian village to global city-state.

Al Ain Souk and Oasis

Heading north-west from the museum you will reach the bus station and the adjacent **Al Ain Souk ❷** (10am–10pm daily), the main meat, fruit and vegetable market, attracting various local characters. A similar experience can be found at the Camel Souk south of the city.

South of the souk (and west of the museum), stretches the idyllic **Al Ain Oasis ❸** (daily sunrise–sunset; free), the largest of the seven oases scattered across the city. Various entrances lead into the oasis, with a network of narrow, shaded lanes running between densely planted areas of palm trees, dotted with fig and banana trees, all of it a pleasant

Al Ain's Eastern Fort

place to enjoy a stroll amid some rare tranquillity right in the city centre, and see and hear the bird and insect life. The plantations are watered using the traditional *falaj* irrigation, with the 3,000 year-old method bringing water via mud-walled channels from where it comes to the surface out of the nearby surrounding mountains.

Al Ain Palace Museum and Jahili Fort

Follow the road around the north side of the oasis to reach the **Al Ain Palace Museum** (www.abudhabi.ae; Sat–Thu 8.30am–7.30pm, closed Mon, Fri 3–7.30pm; free). The sprawling complex has buildings set around courtyards and small gardens, and recreates the home of Sheikh Zayed – prior to 1966 when he moved to Abu Dhabi to become ruler of the UAE – and features background information on the life of the ruling family in the 1940s and 50s.

Nearby stands the **Jahili Fort** (www.abudhabi.ae; Sun–Thu 9am–5pm, Fri 3–5pm, closed Mon; free), one of the finest traditional buildings in Al Ain, built in 1898 and the birthplace

of Sheikh Zayed. There is also an excellent exhibition showcasing the photographs of explorer Wilfred Thesiger (1910–2003), who stayed at the fort in the late 1940s. Head north into the city centre and have lunch at **Al Mallah**, see ❶.

Camel Souk

The new **Camel Souk** (www.visitabu dhabi.ae) is worth a visit if you're in town in time, with its lively crowd haggling over the camels and other livestock. The souk

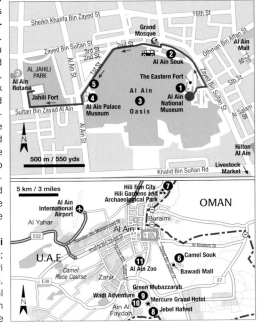

Local man with camel   *On the road to the summit of Jebel Hafeet*

is busiest before 10am, although low-key trading sometimes continues during the day. To reach the souk, take the road to the east of Al Ain Oasis (Zayed Bin Sultan St) straight over the roundabout by the Hilton hotel and south towards Mazyad. After about 3km (2 miles), the souk is past the mall on the left.

Hili Archaeological Park & Hili Fun City

On the northern side of the city, the **Al Hili Archaeological Park** ❼ (www.abud-habi.ae; daily 9am–10pm) is one of the most important archaeological sites in the UAE. Many buildings and tombs have been uncovered, dating from as early as 5,000 years ago, with some now restored to illustrate life in the Umm Al Nar period (2700–2000 BC). The Great Hili Tomb, from the 3rd century BC, is decorated with primitive carvings.

Jebel Hafeet

Some 30km (18.6 miles) south of Al Ain, right on the border with Oman, rises **Jebel Hafeet** ❽ (1,180m/3,870ft), the second highest mountain in the UAE. With a good tarmac road all the way up, it's about a half-hour drive to the top, with glorious views; the terrace at the Mercure Grand hotel, just below the summit, makes a memorable – if surprisingly chilly – spot for a drink or bite to eat on the outdoor terrace.

At the foot of the mountain, **Green Mubazzarah** ❾ offers a park, chalets, camping and other facilities in an extraordinary landscape of grass-covered hills, man-made trickling streams and hot springs. Located right next to Jebel Hafeet, it is worth stopping by on the way up or down. The newest attraction in this area is **Wadi Adventure** ❿ (www.wadi adventure.ae; 10am–7pm), where you can surf an artificial break, kayak or raft down white-water rapids, try cable-pulled wakeboarding or enjoy a dip at the 'Open Beach' swimming sessions or in the pool.

Al Ain Zoo

On your way back into town from Jebel Hafeet, **Al Ain Zoo** ⓫ (www.alainzoo.ae; Sat–Wed 9am–8pm, Thu–Fri 9am–9pm) is by far the best animal attraction in the UAE, and has recently been added to with the Sheikh Zayed Desert Learning Centre and the Al Ain Safari – a private tour by 4WD or truck with an Emirati tour guide around the world's largest man-made safari park with more than 200 African animals in natural surroundings. With all the animals in great condition and kept in well-designed environments, you will need at least half a day to get around it all.

Food and drink

❶ AL MALLAH

Just south of Globe Roundabout, northern edge of Al Ain city centre; daily 10am–midnight; $

A popular Lebanese café, good for inexpensive but tasty fare, including shawarmas and fruit juices. No alcohol.

The road from Masafi to Dibba

THE EAST COAST

*The east coast of the UAE offers a rewarding escape from the busy cities
in the west, with wild mountains, history and heritage, deserted beaches,
diving and snorkelling just off-shore, and a pleasantly slower pace of life.*

DISTANCE: 212km (132 miles) round trip
TIME: A full day
START/END: Dubai

POINTS TO NOTE: A rental car (see page 130) is required for this route, although if you don't fancy driving, many tour operators in Dubai offer 'East Coast Tours' that cover most or all of the places below.

The eastern coast of the UAE offers a striking contrast to Dubai, its craggy coastline, deserted beaches and dramatic wadis are all barely touched by tourism. Along the Gulf of Oman, a string of quiet towns dot the coast, backed by the rocky Hajar Mountains, and secluded and largely deserted beaches lie between. The beach resorts of Al Aqah are a popular weekend retreat for Dubai expats.

EAST TO MASAFI

From Dubai, it's a two-hour drive to Al Aqah, on the coast north of Fujairah city. For the first part of the journey, take the E44 out of Dubai (east), then turn north onto the E611 (Emirates Road) to the Sharjah–Dhaid road (E88), then follow the signs east to Al Dhaid.

At Junction 8 of the Sharjah-Al Dhaid road you pass **Sharjah Desert Park** ❶ (www.epaashj.ae; Sun–Thu 9am–5.30pm, closed Tue, Sat 11am–5.30pm, Fri 2–5.30pm). The park houses the interesting Sharjah Natural History Museum, an Islamic botanical garden, a children's farm and the Arabian Wildlife Centre – a large collection of Arabian wildlife either located indoors, or in outdoor areas you can view from air-conditioned comfort indoors.

At Al Dhaid, a small oasis town that is kept green by ancient *falaj* channels fed by mountain springs, follow the signs to Masafi and Fujairah.

MASAFI

The scenery now starts to change from rocky plains to mountains. In a small gorge about 5km (3 miles) before reaching the modest little town of **Masafi** ❷ – perhaps best known

Pottery at the Friday Market

as the source of the popular brand of UAE mineral water – you'll find the lively 'Friday Market' (actually open all week, despite its name). The long string of shops lining both sides of the main road sell fresh produce, souvenirs and handicrafts including ornamental pots, plants, and huge quantities of carpets, although most are machine-made, and of low quality.

Head left at the large roundabout in the centre of Masafi, following the signs for Dibba and Al Aqah. From here the road rises and falls through striking mountain scenery before passing south of Dibba town.

DIBBA

Nestled below the mountains at the southern end of the Musandam Peninsula, **Dibba** ❸ is actually three towns in one. The largest part of town belongs to the emirate of Fujairah; next to this is a smaller area administered by Sharjah, and Dibba Bayah (or Daba), is actually in Oman. Though isolated, this area has a rich history: in 633ad the Muslim forces

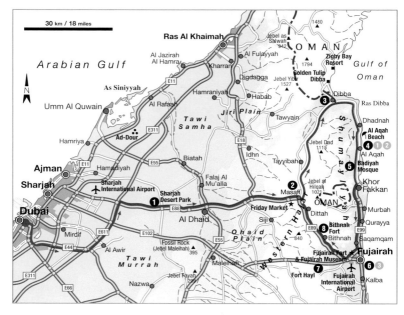

Fishermen in Dibba

of Caliph Abu Baker waged a battle on this spot to suppress a rebellion and claim the Arabian peninsula for Islam.

Dibba itself is one of the more pleasant towns in the UAE, although there's not much to see from a tourist point of view apart from a couple of large mosques on the seafront corniche, each sporting a quartet of minarets, and the quirky sequence of oversized sculptures which adorn the town's various roundabouts (including a monster coffeepot, oil lamp and a pile of earthenware pottery).

Into Oman
It used to be possible to make a side trip north over the border into Omani territory, with no documentation required, but rules have now been tightened up and tourists need their passports, and possibly also printed proof of a reservation for one of the hotels there, otherwise you may not be permittted to cross. If you do gain access, the Omani part of town itself is pleasantly sleepy, fringed with a fine swathe of sand – the northern-most beach next to the rocks past the Golden Tulip is a popular place for day trippers – and the coast is dotted with fishing boats, often with considerable quantities of fish laid out to dry on the sand. Just inland lies the town's impressive fort (signposted as 'Daba Castle') – a fine example of traditional Omani architecture. The hotels in Dibba include the basic **Golden Tulip Dibba** (www.goldentulipdibba.com/en) right on the beachfront, and the luxury – and very expensive – traditionally styled eco-resort of **Six Senses Zighy Bay Resort** (www.sixsenses.com).

Al Aqah Beach
Heading south from Dibba, following the signs along the coast to Fujairah, you will pass several smaller hotels before reaching reach **Al Aqah Beach** ❹ after around 15km (9 miles), a recently developed area that is home to several popular resort hotels which attract hordes of visiting Dubaians during the weekend (although things are quieter during the week). The major landmark is the towering **Le Meridien Al Aqah** (www.le meridien-alaqah.com), an incongruously grand structure which looks like it's been airlifted straight from Dubai Marina. Just next door stands the equally vast, but low-rise **Fujairah Rotana** (www.rotana. com), and a little further south, the **Miramar Al Aqah Beach** (www.miramar alaqah.com), a luxury Arabian-style resort. A short distance from these upmarket options, the **Sandy Beach Motel** (www.sandybm.com) is a more budget beach hotel boasting unbeatable prime access to the snorkelling around Snoopy Island – named after its supposed resemblance to Snoopy from the Peanuts comic strip by Charles Schulz, and a must see for the chance to get up close to a wide variety of marine life, including shoals of colourful fish, plus maybe also sharks, turtles and cuttlefish. Day visitors can use the facilities for a fee, including hiring snorkelling gear.

Zighy Bay *Badiyah Mosque*

All hotels offer an appealing spot to hole up for a night or two, enjoying the fine wide beach and the swimming and snorkelling in the unspoilt coastal waters, and there's a range of dining options for grabbing lunch, including the attractive **The Views** at the five-star Le Meridien Al Aqah, see ①, or the cheap and cheerful café style eateries at Sandy Beach, such as **Snoopy's Pool Bar & Grill**, see ②.

BADIYAH AND KHOR FAKKAN

Continuing along the coast towards Fujairah city, it's around 8km (5 miles) to the tiny, historic 15th-century **Badiyah Mosque** ❺ (daily 24hrs; free), the oldest mosque in the UAE, on the right of the road. Non-Muslims may be permitted inside (outside of prayer times) for a glimpse of the atmospheric interior, and there are stunning views of the sea and mountains from the watchtower on the hill above.

A further 10km (6 miles) down the road, the small port of **Khor Fakkan** (actually part of the emirate of Sharjah) is the next major town along the coast, with a seafront corniche spread along a handsome stretch of coast.

FUJAIRAH CITY

Even the low-key high-rises and modest urban sprawl of **Fujairah City** ❻ can come as something of a surprise after the undeveloped countryside further up the coast. Most of the city's new-found wealth is thanks to its huge port, from which most of the UAE's oil is exported – long lines of tankers can usually be seen queuing offshore.

Oil aside, the main attractions in the city are **Fujairah Fort** (tel: 09 222 9085; Sun–Thu 9am–6pm, Fri & Sat 3–6pm; free) and close by, **Fujairah Museum** (details as above; but entry is Dhs.5), both in the northwest of the city. Dating back 500 years in places, the fort is the oldest in the UAE and perhaps the most

Bullfighting

Traditional Arab sports such as falconry and camel racing are not suited to the terrain of the east coast. As a result, the large Brahmin bull, which has worked for centuries in the area's palm groves, is bred to compete. The contest is between two large, pampered bulls, each weighing a tonne (ton) or more and fed on a diet of milk, honey and meal. Not the same as bull-fights in Europe, these bouts are decided when the two bulls try to force each other to the ground. Winners are also declared if an opposing bull turns and flees. The sport was possibly introduced in the 16th century by the Portuguese, although it may also pre-date Islam with its source in Persia, where the bull was once worshipped. The contests are held on Friday afternoons in winter, in special arenas on the road heading south to Kalba out of Fujairah city.

Bullfight prepration in the city of Fujairah

impressive, set against a stunning mountain backdrop, and fun to explore. The nearby museum gives a lot of insight into the history of this part of the country with a variety of well-thought out exhibits.

If you want something to eat before turning back to Dubai, head for the Hilton Fujairah on the coast and visit **Breezes Beach Bar & Terrace**, see ③.

Bithnah Fort & Fort Hayl

From Fujairah, the route home follows the signs to Masafi then retraces your steps back west through the desert. Just outside the city, a short drive into the mountains takes you to the secluded **Fort Hayl** ⑦, a small fort in a rare hidden location, guarding a *wadi*. Further towards Masafi, some 15km (9 miles) from Fujairah City, the quiet village of Bithnah is home to the atmospheric old **Bithnah Fort** ⑧ to the right of the highway as it twists and turns through the mountains. Set above the village, you can climb up through the fort for some nice views over the sprawling oasis.

Off the beaten track

This part of the UAE has dozens of off-road routes that take you on winding tracks into the *wadis* and mountains to visit shady streams and pools, hidden forts, breezy hill-top plateaus for camping or lunch breaks with stunning views, rare patches of lush greenery in tucked-away palm tree oases and farms, and hikes on Bedu paths up to several thousand metres above sea level. Some of these can be done accessed by two-wheel-drive, others need a 4WD to tackle the rugged terrain. If you want to get a bit more 'out there' and explore this hidden side of Arabia, pick up a copy of *UAE Off-Road* (Explorer Publishing), for details of what routes are on offer, and exactly how to navigate them.

Food and drink

① THE VIEWS

Le Meridien Al Aqah Beach Resort, Al Aqah; tel: 09 244 9000; www.lemeridien-alaqah.com; open 24hr; $$$
Luxurious lunch-stop at this five-star resort, to enjoy fine sea views and international food from the brasserie-style menu.

② SNOOPY'S POOL BAR & GRILL

Sandy Beach Hotel, Al Aqah; tel: 09 244 5555; www.sandybeachhotel.ae; 10am–9pm; $$
In contrast to the five-star resorts, Sandy Beach's diners offer more low-key, casual and homely venues for lunch, with views out to Snoopy Island and access to all the facilities.

③ BREEZES BEACH BAR AND TERRACE

Hilton Fujairah Resort, Fujairah City; tel: 09 222 2411; daily 11am–midnight; $$$
Pleasant al fresco spot for lunch or an early dinner before heading back to Dubai, with sea views from the garden setting, and a wide international menu.

Sheikh Zayed Grand Mosque

ABU DHABI

The wealthier and more sedate capital of the UAE is an interesting contrast to its glitzy neighbour, Dubai. Abu Dhabi doesn't disappoint, however, and you'll find it has its own fair share of beautiful beaches and swanky hotels, as well as some of the country's landmark attractions.

DISTANCE: 238km (147 miles) round trip
TIME: A full day
START/END: Abu Dhabi
POINTS TO NOTE: Regular buses to Abu Dhabi depart from Al Ghubaiba Bus Station in Bur Dubai every 30 minutes between 5.30am and 11.30pm (Dhs20 one way), although given that the journey can take around two hours or longer, this makes for a very long day trip. Taxis are a more expensive option (Dhs250 one way). Ideally, it's worth renting a car, which will get you to Abu Dhabi much quicker than the bus and will also allow you to get around the various sights (which are widely spread out) without constantly jumping in and out of cabs. The drive is straightforward and quick (around 1hr 30mins each way) – follow the Abu Dhabi signs along Sheikh Zayed Road (E11).

In the past Abu Dhabi, the federal capital of the UAE, has had a rather cool approach to tourism, and tourists have been equally cool in return. With more than 94 percent of the UAE's oil reserves (some 10 percent of the world's total), the emirate hasn't needed to diversify its economy and rely on tourism in the way that Dubai has. The city is slowly waking up to the benefits of tourism, however, with a string of ongoing mega-developments aimed at raising its global profile.

Located on an island, Abu Dhabi is accessed via the Al Maqta Bridge. The old watchtower, which is visible from the bridge, can be seen in early black-and-white photographs of the city, when camel trains crossed from the mainland to the island at low tide.

QASR AL HOSN

The historic heart of the city is **Qasr Al Hosn** ❶ (aka Al Hosn Palace or White Fort; tel: 02 697 6472), located on Khaled Bin Al Waleed Street, a couple of blocks from the corniche at the top of the island. The oldest building in Abu Dhabi, it was built in 1793, the year the city was established, and was the residence of the ruling Al Nahyan

On the Corniche

family before finally becoming a visitor attraction. The original fort was built to protect the town's well, and the outer walls and tower were added at a later date. Today, its ancient battlements stand in stark contrast to the high-rise offices, apartments and hotels that surround it. The fort is still being renovated (completion date estimated as 2017 at the time of writing) and the only time you can access it is during the Qasr Al Hosn Festival (www. qasralhosnfestival.ae), held every year in February. Outside of these times, there is an exhibition centre next to the fort which is worth a visit. The nearby **Abu Dhabi Cultural Foundation**, previously the city's arts centre, is now, like the fort, currently closed while it is being redeveloped. The ever-popular **Lebanese Flower** restaurant, see ❶, is close to Al Hosn, and a great place to stop for lunch.

THE CORNICHE

A short walk along Khaled Bin Al Waleed Street leads to the 8km (5-

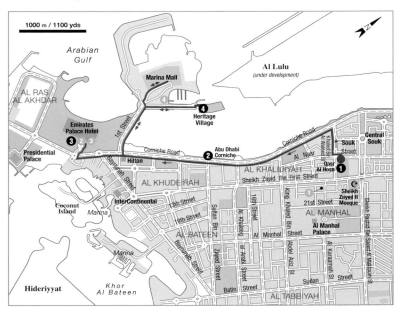

Emirates Palace Hotel

Inside Sheikh Zayed Grand Mosque

mile) -long **Abu Dhabi Corniche** ➋ (www.visitabudhabi.ae), the longest in the UAE. The best time to visit is late afternoon (or Fridays and weekends in the winter), when the population of Abu Dhabi seems to head down here to stroll, play on the golden beaches or jog through the breezy gardens lining the waterfront. The several nearby parks are packed with kite-flyers on Fridays and public holidays.

Emirates Palace Hotel

At the west end of the island, the corniche continues towards the presidential palace and the landmark **Emirates Palace Hotel** ➌, one of the most opulent in the world. Constructed in traditional Arabian style, this red-sand-stone colossus sprawls for the best part of a kilometre (0.6 miles) down the beach, topped with around a hundred domes, while the interior is a riot of Arabian chintz, best appreciated over afternoon tea in the foyer at **Le Café**, see ➋. It's also a great place to enjoy an upmarket dinner – **Mezzaluna**, see ➌, offers good Italian food, and is not too pricey.

On the Breakwater near Marina Mall is the **Heritage Village** ➍ (http://torath.ae; Sat–Thu 9am–5pm, Fri 3.30–9pm; free), which illustrates the history of the emirate before oil revenues transformed the landscape. There is an exhibition of a Bedouin camp, a reconstruction of a palm house, an old fishing village, and traditional crafts

and souks. In addition, it offers a fabulous view of the Abu Dhabi skyline across the water. The **Havana Café**, see ➍, is nearby.

FURTHER OUT

As Abu Dhabi's development gathers pace, some of the biggest modern landmarks lie across the water from the main island, while there's also the grand mosque at the southern end of the island.

Sheikh Zayed Grand Mosque

Some 10km (6.2 miles) from the city centre, close to Al Maqta Bridge, the monumental **Sheikh Zayed Grand Mosque** ➎ (www.szgmc.ae; Sat–Thu 9am–10pm, Fri 4.30–10pm; interior closed for prayer times at 12.30pm, 3.30pm, 6pm & 7.30pm.,free guided tours; free) rises imperiously over the city. This is undoubtedly Abu Dhabi's single most worthwhile attraction: a spectacular, snow-white mass of domes and minarets visible for miles around; the vast courtyard alone is capable of accommodating some 40,000 worshippers.

Completed in 2007, this is one of the world's biggest mosques – and certainly the most expensive, having cost some $500 million. It's also one of only two mosques in the UAE (along with the Jumeira Mosque in Dubai; see page 55) open to non-Muslims. If visiting, you'll be expected to dress

Practice ahead of the Abu Dhabi Formula One Grand Prix at Yas Marina Circuit

conservatively; female visitors not suitably attired will be offered a black *abaya* to wear.

Yas Island

Some 20km (12.4 miles) from the city centre, just offshore from the highway to Dubai, **Yas Island ⑥** (www. yasisland.ae) is one of Abu Dhabi's newest developed areas, home to the Yas Marina Circuit Formula 1 racetrack, venue for the Abu Dhabi Grand Prix (www.yasmarinacircuit.com/en/formula-1/2016-grand-prix), which

has been the final race in the F1 season since 2010.

The island also has the state-of-the-art **Ferrari World Abu Dhabi** theme park (https://ferrariworldabudhabi. com; daily 11am–8pm), the largest indoor theme park featuring over 20 rides and attractions including the world's fastest rollercoaster and F1 racing simulators, plus plenty more sedate family rides and kids' attractions; and Yas Waterworld (https://yaswaterworld.com) one of the top waterparks in the world, built with an

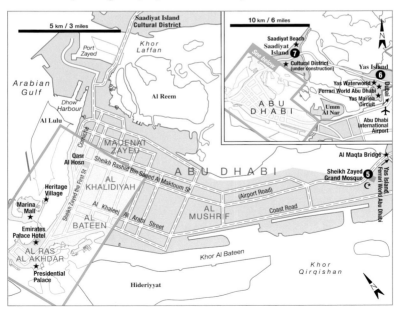

Ferrari Museum at Ferrari World

Emirati theme, offering everything from high-octane looping waterslide and tornados to family-friendly fun.

Saadiyat Island

Foremost amongst Abu Dhabi's planned mega-projects is the massive **Saadiyat Island** development ❼, a short hop across the new bridge from the city centre. The island will feature the Saadiyat Cultural District (www.saadiyatculturaldistrict.ae), already home to several art galleries, and will eventually have an unprecedented number of institutions by world-famous architects, including a branch of the Guggenheim museum designed by Frank Gehry (opening late 2017); the Louvre Abu Dhabi (http://louvre abudhabi.ae/en) by French architect Jean Nouvel, due to be open by 2017; and Zayed National Museum (www.zayednationalmuseum.ae), a new national museum for the UAE by British architect Norman Foster, opening in late 2016. Already open on the island are several five-star hotels, the private Saadiyat Beach Club, and a public beach, with more are opening all the time.

Food and drink

❶ LEBANESE FLOWER

Off 26th Street, near Al Hosn; tel 02 665 8700; $$

An Abu Dhabi institution, tucked away in a side street near Al Hosn, this Lebanese restaurant is the best place in the city to fill up on inexpensive Middle Eastern food, with an excellent selection of grills, kebabs and mezze.

❷ LE CAFÉ

Emirates Palace Hotel, Corniche West Street; tel: 02 690 7999; www.kempinski.com; daily 6.30am–1am; $$$

The café in the foyer of the opulent Emirates Palace Hotel provides a sumptuous setting for a memorable – if expensive – high tea, served from 4–7pm daily.

❸ MEZZALUNA

Emirates Palace Hotel, Corniche West Street; 02 690 7999; www.kempinski.com; daily 12.30–3pm and 7–11pm; $$$$

This is the place to come for a slice of opulence (and it is less expensive than other restaurants in the hotel), with superb traditional Italian and Mediterranean dishes.

❹ HAVANA CAFÉ

Near Marina Mall, Breakwater; tel: 02 681 0044; daily 9am–2am; $$

The mainly Arabic menu also includes international fare such as sandwiches and pizza. Patio and rooftop seating are available in the cooler months, with excellent views across the Abu Dhabi waterfront to the high rises along the Corniche.

Flamingoes at Ras Al Khor

OUTLYING AREAS

With Dubai being so spread out – and the master plan still having so many unconnected gaps in it at present – heading out of the main city gets you to the outer fringes, home to some of the biggest projects and attractions, as well as some really unique and interesting places to see.

DISTANCE/TIME: As little or as much as you'd like
START/END: Wherever you like
POINTS TO NOTE: Hiring a car for a day to brave the roads (quieter outside the city centre) would be an essential way to travel if you plan to link up a few of these places in a day. If you really don't want to drive and want to be chauffeured around, you can rent a taxi for 6 or 12 hours from Dubai Taxi (www.dubaitaxi.ae). One possible route would include Ras Al Khor Wildlife Sanctuary, Falcon and Heritage Sports Centre, Al Quoz Art District, Dubai Miracle Garden and Global Village, the five of which would make for a packed full, really fun and varied day out. The theme parks could easily fill up a day each.

Below are descriptions of some of the best spots to visit, located on the map, but in no particular order; just head for what you like the sound of and make a day of it!

DUBAI PARKS & RESORTS

With confidence in Dubai growing again, especially in the build up to Expo 2020, the end of 2016 saw the opening of the first significantly sized leisure attraction in a while with **Dubai Parks & Resorts** ❶ (www.dubaiparksandresorts.com). This collection of theme parks include Motiongate Dubai, with five areas representing DreamWorks, Sony Studios and Lionsgate, as well as Smurfs Village; LEGOLAND Dubai; LEGOLAND Water Park; Bollywood Parks Dubai, a one of a kind park featuring attractions based on Bollywood hit moves; the Lapita Hotel Dubai, a family resort; and a massive area full of dining options known as Riverland. As the parks weren't open at the time of writing, visit the website to see further information on all the parks have to offer.

PALM JEBEL ALI

Built at the height of Dubai's ambition, **Palm Jebel Ali** ❷ saw the pre-selling of large parts of the development and the construction of an even larger island

Ibn Battuta Mall

than the (nearly complete) Palm Jumeirah before the economic crash forced its developers to mothball the project in 2008. Years later, there are still no plans to restart work on it, and it's just a case of wait and see for when (or if?) things get rolling again.

IBN BATTUTA MALL

One of Dubai's most unique shopping centres, and billed as the world's largest theme mall, **Ibn Battuta Mall ❸** (www.ibnbattutamall.com; daily 10am–10pm, Wed–Fri until midnight), is situated in something of a no-man's land at the far southern end of the city, close to the industrial works and container docks of the Jebel Ali Free Trade Zone. The mall is one of the city's most outlandish but engaging attractions, inspired by the travels of the famous Moroccan wanderer Ibn Battuta, with different sections themed after six of the many countries and regions he visited – Morocco, Andalucia, Tunisia, Persia, India and China – all designed with Dubai's characteristic mix of whimsy, extravagance and high-end kitsch. 2016 saw the opening of a large extension, with 60 new shops, a link to the metro station and the first hotel at the mall. More is also planned for the next five years.

DUBAILAND

Some 10km (6.2 miles) inland from Dubai Marina lies the proposed site of the vast new **Dubailand ❹** development. Launched in 2003, Dubailand was originally planned to be nothing less than the world's largest and most spectacular tourist development, with a mind-boggling mix of theme parks and sporting and leisure facilities – twice the size of the Walt Disney World Resort in Florida.

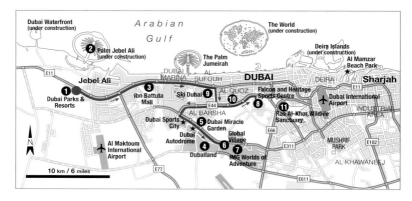

Extraordinary floral art at Dubai Miracle Garden

Parts of complex are already open, including the Dubai Autodrome and Dubai Sports City, complete with an international cricket stadium and several golf courses. Work on other projects, however, came to an end indefinitely in the economic slowdown of 2008. Some movement has been made to start development (see Dubai Miracle Garden), but whether any of Dubailand's more ambitious projects will now ever see the light of day is anyone's guess.

Dubai Miracle Garden

One of the only openings in the Dubailand area recently, the **Dubai Miracle Garden** ❺ (Shk Mohd Rd, near Dubai Autodrome; 04 422 8902; www.dubaimiraclegarden. com; daily 9am–9pm, Fri/Sat until 11pm, closed during summer) is the world's biggest flower garden, with nearly 50 million flowers arranged in surreal, spectacular displays to wander around and absorb, more of a mega art installation than your typical garden. While you're in the area (accessible by bus, or a short ten minute car or taxi ride from Mall of The Emirates), the perfect companion for the Miracle Garden is the **Dubai Butterfly Garden** (www.dubaibutterflygarden.com, same timings and location as above), which charges separately for entry, and offers the chance to walk through temperature controlled domes that are home to thousands of butterflies from 32 species, which flutter around you, even landing on an outstretched hand. Definitely worth the money for the experience.

GLOBAL VILLAGE

Situated in the outskirts of Dubai, on Sheikh Mohammed Bin Zayed Road near Arabian Ranches, **Global Village** ❻ is a permanent festival site open from November through to April every evening from 4pm till late. Hundreds of international pavilions have stalls selling traditional items from many countries around the world, while a vast array of restaurants and stalls sell all types of food, including chances to try some lesser-known cuisines. There are rides for all ages in Fantasy Island, plus events such as stunt shows, magic and concerts, and fireworks every night, which make for a fun-packed evening. Entry is only Dhs15, and you pay for all attractions separately.

IMG Worlds of Adventure Dubai

Opened in summer 2016, **IMG Worlds of Adventure** ❼ (Shk Mohd Bin Zayed Rd, next to Global Village; www.img worlds.com; daily 12pm–8pm) is the largest indoor theme park in the world. Designed to fill a gap for people in the Middle East and Asia, it aims to make it more accessible to visit a world-class theme park. Areas in the gigantic air-conditioned building include Marvel Zone, Cartoon Network Zone, and Lost Valley, the Dinosaur Adventure zone – home to a number of wild rides through the jungle inhabited by 70 realistic animatronic dinosaurs. Tickets start at Dhs250 and include all rides.

Ski Dubai, why not?

The India pavilion at Global Village

FALCON AND HERITAGE SPORTS CENTRE

Offering an insight into a rare part of Arabic culture, the **Falcon and Heritage Sports Centre** ❽ (Nad Al Sheba; www.dm.gov.ae; Sun–Thu 7am–6pm; free) is free to visit, with guided tours also complimentary. There are birds on show, falconry displays, a centre for those buying and selling falcons and accessories, and displays of the history of falconry and how important a part it is of Emirati culture. Busiest during winter.

SKI DUBAI

As you near Mall of the Emirates, the huge dome of **Ski Dubai** ❾ (www.theplaymania.com/skidubai; Sun–Wed 10am–11pm, Thu until midnight, Fri 9am–midnight, Sat 9am–11pm) looms, and is home to chairlifts and a 400m (1,312ft) ski-slope, ski and snowboard lessons, a fun snow park for all ages, the Snow Bullet zipline, chalet rooms overlooking the slopes from the Kempinski hotel, and a group of resident penguins. Definitely something unique for anyone's visit to the Middle East! Clothing hire is included, but gloves are extra.

AL QUOZ ART DISTRICT

Over the last twenty years, **Al Quoz** ❿, one of Dubai's industrial areas, has seen the emergence of a small art scene bubbling up to the surface. Not as planned as others in Dubai and Abu Dhabi, artists have tended to gather here organically, creating several areas, some located together in warehouses that are home to collections of galleries such as **Alserkal Avenue** (http://alserkalavenue.ae) and **The Courtyard** (www.courtyard-uae.com), as well as many other smaller independent galleries, including **The Third Line** (www.thethirdline.com). These galleries cluster together a short way back from Sheikh Zayed Road, between Times Square shopping mall and the Al Manara interchange. Several of Dubai's coolest cafés have also opened up here.

RAS AL KHOR WILDLIFE SANCTUARY

Located right in the city centre at the inland end of Dubai Creek, this surprising **sanctuary** ⓫ (www.dm.gov.ae Sat–Thu 9am–4pm; free) is a protected site and a wetland of importance in the UAE. Three viewing hides allow you to watch the variety of birdlife that stop here on their annual migration, including the famous flamingos, which feed in the shallow waters. Perhaps the best hide is one of the two on the west side of the sanctuary on the Dubai–Al Ain Road (E66), the third is on the south side on the Ras Al Khor Road (E44) – to get here you'll need to do an 8km (5 miles) loop back around to the correct side of the highway. Wardens are sometimes on hand to offer some information on what you can see, and often lend you binoculars or telescopes.

UNIQUE EXPERIENCES

Atlantis The Palm

The colossal hotel at end of the man-made Palm Jumeirah is one of Dubai's most glamorous and extravagant destinations. The resort is visited on route 6 offering chic restaurants and bars, and the magnificent water park, Aquaventure.

Desert adventure

A bumpy ride through the desert, sailing over huge sand dunes in a 4x4, and pitching up a tent for the night before settling down to a traditional Arabian meal, is an experience not to be missed in the UAE, see route 8.

Al Fahidi Historical Neighbourhood

The wind towers of Al Fahidi Historical Neighbourhood, with its quiet walkways and traditional buildings, feel a world away from other parts of Dubai. Route 1 takes you through this atmospheric heritage area, which is home to the popular XVA Gallery.

Dubai Creek

A visit to the busy Creek area is one of Dubai's truly original experiences. Route 7 suggests ways to tour the waterway by *abra*, *dhow* cruise or water taxi.

WALKING EYE
Mobile App

DUBAI

FREE EBOOK
WITH THIS GUIDE

This Explore now includes a free eBook for the same great price. Find out how to download yours on page 3 inside.

Best routes

Detailed itineraries feature all the best places to visit, including where to eat and drink along the way

Insider recommendations

What to see and do whatever your interest, and what not to miss while you're there

Hand-picked places

Find your way to great hotels, restaurants and nightlife using the comprehensive listings

Informative tips

Plan your visit with an A to Z of advice on everything from transport to tipping

Practical maps

Get around with ease and follow the routes with the free pull-out map

£8.99

ISBN 978-178-671-534-0

51299

US$12.99

Find out more about the UAE at
www.insightguides.com/UAE

MAP LEGEND

●	Start of tour	
→	Tour & route direction	
❶	Recommended sight	
❷	Recommended restaurant/café	
★	Place of interest	
❶	Tourist information	
✈	Airport	
▬▬	Railway	
- - -	Ferry route	
Ⓜ	Metro station	
○	Tram line / station	
🏛	Museum or gallery	
🚹	Statue/monument	
✉	Main post office	
🚌	Bus station	
⛴	Abra station (water taxi)	
☪	Mosque	
🗼	Lighthouse	
⚑	Beach	
※	Viewpoint	
🜨	Cave	
▲	Summit	
∴	Ancient Site	
	Important building	
	Hotel	
	Pedestrian area	
	Shop / market	
	Park	
	Urban area	
	National Park	
— · —	National boundary	

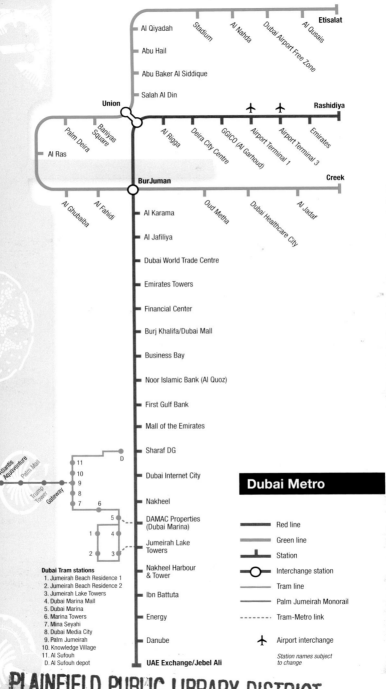

Al Qiyadah
Abu Hail
Abu Baker Al Siddique
Salah Al Din

Union

Stadium
Al Nahda
Dubai Airport Free Zone
Al Qusais

Etisalat

Rashidiya

Palm Deira
Baniyas Square
Al Ras
Al Rigga
Deira City Centre
GGICO (Al Garhoud)
Airport Terminal 1
Airport Terminal 3
Emirates

BurJuman

Creek

Al Ghubaiba
Al Fahidi
Oud Metha
Dubai Healthcare City
Al Jadaf

Al Karama
Al Jafiliya
Dubai World Trade Centre
Emirates Towers
Financial Center
Burj Khalifa/Dubai Mall
Business Bay
Noor Islamic Bank (Al Quoz)
First Gulf Bank
Mall of the Emirates
Sharaf DG
Dubai Internet City
Nakheel
DAMAC Properties (Dubai Marina)
Jumeirah Lake Towers
Nakheel Harbour & Tower
Ibn Battuta
Energy
Danube

UAE Exchange/Jebel Ali

Atlantis
Aquaventure
Palm Mall
Trump Tower
Gateway

11
10
9
8
7
6
5
1
4
2
3
D

Dubai Tram stations
1. Jumeirah Beach Residence 1
2. Jumeirah Beach Residence 2
3. Jumeirah Lake Towers
4. Dubai Marina Mall
5. Dubai Marina
6. Marina Towers
7. Mina Seyahi
8. Dubai Media City
9. Palm Jumeirah
10. Knowledge Village
11. Al Sufouh
D. Al Sufouh depot

Dubai Metro

▬▬▬	Red line
▬▬▬	Green line
┳	Station
◯	Interchange station
▬▬▬	Tram line
▬▬▬	Palm Jumeirah Monorail
- - - -	Tram-Metro link
✈	Airport interchange

Station names subject to change

DIRECTORY

Hand-picked hotels and restaurants to suit all budgets and tastes, organised by area, plus select nightlife listings, an alphabetical listing of practical information, a language guide and an overview of the best books and films to give you a flavour of the city.

Hilton Dubai Creek pool

ACCOMMODATION

Dubai's hotels are not cheap, and the best deals are likely to be found through tour operators in your country of origin during the northern hemisphere summer. If you call hotels direct, most quoted room rates will not include 20 per cent tax and service charge or breakfast. The majority of less expensive hotels can be found in Bur Dubai and Deira, while the most desirable upmarket properties (with a few notable exceptions) are on Sheikh Zayed Road and along the coast. Stretching from Jumeira through Umm Suqeim to Al Sufouh and Al Mina Al Seyahi, the coast is commonly referred to as 'Jumeira'. It may seem some distance on maps, but the hotels in this area are actually only 30 minutes' drive from the airport. If you choose to book into a landlocked hotel in the city, ask if it has a sister hotel on the coast with beachside facilities that you are entitled to use.

The price indicator after each listing is based on two people sharing a standard double room for one night in high season (Nov–April) with tax and service charges included.
$$$$ = More than US$1,000
$$$ = US$500–1,000
$$ = US$250–500
$ = Less than US$250

Bur Dubai

Arabian Courtyard
Al Fahidi St; tel 04 351 9111, www.arabian courtyard.com; $$
Overlooking Dubai Museum, this attractive four-star hotel could hardly be more central or better positioned for forays into the old city centre. Inside the hotel, there are attractive rooms decorated with Arabian touches and some good eating and drinking options.

Four Points Sheraton Bur Dubai
Khalid Bin Al Waleed Street; tel: 04 397 7444; www.fourpoints.com/burdubai; $$
Right in the heart of the old city, this comfortable and competitively priced four-star hotel makes an excellent base for exploring Bur Dubai and Deira and boasts good facilities including the lovely Antique Bazaar Indian restaurant and the cosy Viceroy Pub.

Golden Sands
Al Mankhool Road; tel: 04 355 5553; www.goldensandsdubai.com; $$
A vast number of pleasant self-catering studios and apartments scattered over 11 separate buildings in the Al Mankhool area of Bur Dubai – often some of the cheapest lodgings in town, if you don't mind forgoing some hotel facilities.

XVA Art Hotel
Al Fahidi Historical Neighbourhood; tel: 04

Hyatt Regency Dubai exterior

353 5383; www.xvahotel.com; $

No other accommodation in Dubai can compete with the XVA's authentic Arabian offering. More guesthouse than hotel – the XVA is an art gallery in the courtyard of a restored home in the historic Bastakiya district, which has eight guest rooms on the first-floor rooftop, furnished in the Arabian-style, that offer wonderful views of the Creek skyline and nearby wind towers.

Deira

Dubai Youth Hostel

Al Nahda Rd, Al Qusais; tel: 04 298 8151; www.uaeyha.com; $$

Budget accommodation within easy reach of the airport, and of Sharjah, Dubai's youth hotel offers the chance to stay for cheap and meet like-minded travellers. Nearby are a lot of options for eating out and tourist attractions.

Hilton Dubai Creek

Baniyas Road; tel: 04 227 1111; www.hilton.co.uk/dubaicreek; $$

A pared down, but stylish hotel, designed by architect Carlos Ott with soothingly chic rooms and vast quantities of chrome in the foyer. Selling points include the Glasshouse Brasserie and Table 9 restaurants, and a rooftop pool with stunning views.

Hyatt Regency Dubai

Corniche Street; tel: 04 209 1234; www.dubai.regency.hyatt.com; $$

An imposing monolith dominating the mouth of Dubai Creek, the Hyatt Regency has excellent restaurants, including Al Dawaar, Dubai's only revolving restaurant, and one of the few ice rinks in Dubai. The closest high-quality hotel to Deira's Gold Souk.

Park Hyatt Dubai

Dubai Creek Golf & Yacht Club; tel: 04 602 1234; www.dubai.park.hyatt.com; $$$

Rivalling the nearby Raffles for the title of this end of town's top place to stay, this idyllic city retreat occupies a sprawl of Moroccan-style buildings spread along the Creek between the Dubai Creek and Golf clubs, with gorgeous Arabian styling, lush greenery and superb views.

Radisson Blu Dubai Deira Creek

Baniyas Road, Deira; tel: 04 222 7171; www.radissonblu.com/en/hotel-dubaideiracreek; $$

Formerly the InterContinental, this is the oldest five-star in Dubai and still one of the more appealing options in the old city. The hotel has plush décor, a superb selection of in-house restaurants and a brilliantly central location.

Umm Hurair

Grand Hyatt Dubai

Shk Rashid Rd, Umm Hurair; tel: 04 317 1234; www.dubai.grand.hyatt.com; $$$

The 674-room Grand Hyatt dominates the highway on the Bur Dubai side of Garhoud Bridge near Wafi City. The hotel is centrally located between the air-

Fairmont Dubai suite

port, Deira and Sheikh Zayed Road, has rooms with stunning city views and an excellent spread of quality places to eat.

Raffles Dubai

Shk Rashid Rd, Wafi City; tel: 04 324 8888, www.raffles.com/dubai; $$$

A spectacular hotel (see page 45) housed in a giant pyramid, it is decorated with a mix of quirky Egyptian theming and cool Asian designs. There are superb facilities including huge gardens, a gorgeous spa and excellent restaurants and bars.

Sheikh Zayed Road and Downtown Dubai

Armani Hotel Dubai

Burj Khalifa; tel: 04 888 3888, http://dubai.armanihotels.com; $$$$

Occupying the lower floors of the Burj Khalifa, the world's first Armani hotel offers pretty much the last word in designer minimalism – although prices are less stratospheric than might be expected.

Dusit Thani Dubai

Shk Zayed Rd; tel: 04 343 3333; www.dusit.com/dusitthani/dubai; $$$

A striking landmark on Dubai's main road designed to represent two hands pressed together in the traditional Thai wai greeting. Inside, the Dusit has plenty of understated style and the pretty Benjarong, one of the best Thai restaurants in this part of the city.

Fairmont Dubai

Shk Zayed Rd; tel: 04 332 5555;

www.fairmont.com/dubai; $$$

Located at the northern end of Sheikh Zayed Road, the Fairmont is one of the most luxurious hotels along the road, with plush rooms, a decadent spa and a pair of fourth-floor pools, and the popular Exchange Grill restaurant (see page 111).

Ibis World Trade Centre

Shk Zayed Rd, Trade Centre 2; tel: 04 332 4444; www.ibishotel.com; $$

This simple, but comfortable, four-star hotel is perhaps the best value hotel in the city, although if you want to get a room, book early, rooms can get booked up quickly if there's a big event on at the Dubai International Exhibition Centre next door.

Jumeirah Emirates Towers Hotel

Shk Zayed Rd; tel: 04 330 0000; www.jumeirah.com; $$$

Located in the landmark Emirates Towers, and regularly voted the top business hotel in the Middle East, rooms here have stylish décor and wonderful views. The superb restaurants and bars include Alta Badia and Al Nafoorah (see page 110).

JW Marriott Marquis

Business Bay; tel: 04 414 0000; www.jwmarriottmarquisdubailife.com; $$$$

The world's tallest hotel, the twin towers of the Marquis top out at 355m (1,164ft), providing a stylish and luxury city centre hotel, with 14 dining options and easy access to Downtown Dubai.

View from the Shangri-La

The Palace Downtown Dubai

Mohd Bin Rashid Blvd; tel: 04 428 7888, www.theaddress.com; $$$$

The centrepiece of the atmospheric Old Town development, this sumptuous hotel boasts opulent traditional Arabian styling and awesome views of the adjacent Burj Khalifa and Dubai Fountain.

Shangri-La

Shk Zayed Rd; tel: 04 343 8888; www.shangri-la.com/dubai/shangrila; $$$

A striking hotel on Sheikh Zayed Road, set in a towering, Gotham-esque structure at the southern end of the strip. Inside, the hotel is a model of Zen cool, with beautiful rooms (many of them offering outstanding views) and some excellent restaurants.

Jumeira and Umm Suqeim

Burj Al Arab

Umm Suqeim; tel: 04 301 7777; www.burj-al-arab.com; $$$$

Set on its own island beside the Jumeirah Beach Hotel, the iconic, sail-shaped Burj Al Arab offers the ultimate in luxury. One night in a 225 sq m (2,422 sq ft) 'Panoramic' duplex suite complete with butler service costs around US$1,500. Dining options include must-do's, even if you aren't staying here. Guests are ferried around in a fleet of white Rolls-Royces.

Dubai Marine Beach Resort & Spa

Jumeira Road; tel: 04 346 1111; www.dxbmarine.com; $$$

At the northern end of Jumeira, Dubai Marine is the closest beach resort to the city centre, with attractive rooms in low-rise villas in a landscaped compound fronting on to a small beach. It also has some popular nightspots and restaurants.

Jumeirah Beach Hotel

Umm Suqeim; tel: 04 348 0000; www.jumeirahbeachhotel.com; $$$

Designed to look like a wave, which complements neighbouring Burj Al Arab's 'sail', the 26-storey Jumeirah Beach has 600 sea-facing rooms, a breathtaking atrium, a plethora of restaurants and bars and free access to Wild Wadi Waterpark.

Madinat Jumeirah

Umm Suqeim; tel: 04 366 8888; www.madinatjumeirah.com; $$$

This fabulous Arabian-themed resort located near Burj Al Arab contains three hotels: Al Qasr (The Palace); Mina A'Salam ('Port of Peace'); Al Naseem (a new addition in 2016); as well as villas and summer houses, all within an Arabian Nights fantasy with landscaped gardens, winding waterways and paths, 40 restaurants and bars, plus the Souk Madinat Jumeirah.

Dubai Marina and Palm Jumeirah

Anantara Dubai The Palm

Palm Jumeirah; tel: 04 567 8888; http://dubai-palm.anantara.com; $$$

Recreating a Thai village feel with villas fronting out onto the swimming lagoons or on stilts over the sea, as well as the

Jumeirah Zabeel Saray suite bathroom

standard hotel rooms, this resort is another premier luxury destination on The Palm, offering classic Thai hospitality and service. Restaurants include the stylish Mekong servicing a range of Asian cuisine.

Atlantis The Palm
Palm Jumeirah; tel: 04 426 2000; www.atlantisthepalm.com; $$$$
A vast mega-resort (see page 63) on the breakwater of Palm Jumeirah – easily the most ostentatious place to stay, although not as stylish as other top-end places in the city. The range of facilities, including a waterpark, dolphinarium, huge beach and dozens of restaurants and bars, help to compensate.

Grosvenor House
Dubai Marina; tel: 04 399 8888; www.grosvenorhouse-dubai.com; $$$
One of the Marina's most alluring hotels – guests can share the beach and facilities at nearby Le Royal Meridien Beach Resort – the style is slick urban cool, with some excellent bars and restaurants such as Buddha Bar and the ultrachic Bar 44 (with fantastic views).

Hilton Dubai Jumeirah Resort
Dubai Marina; tel: 04 399 8888; www3.hilton.com; $$$
As well as a beautiful stretch of beach, having JBR's The Beach and The Walk right on the doorstep, as well as Dubai Marina, makes the Hilton popular for the choice of entertainment options, while the dining choices might just keep you at the hotel.

Jumeirah Zabeel Saray
Palm Jumeirah; tel: 04 453 0000; www.jumeirah.com; $$$$
Jumeirah's resort on the outer breakwater of The Palm takes the form of a large opulent palace, with lavish Ottoman styling and a range of beautifully designed rooms and villas, a clutch of excellent eating and drinking venues including MusicHall and Voda Bar, plus one of the best spas in the Middle East, the sumptuous Talise Ottoman Spa.

Le Meridien Mina Seyahi
Al Sufouh; tel: 04 399 3333; www.lemeridien-minaseyahi.com; $$$
A great spot on the beach, popular eating out venues including Barasti Bar, close to the attractions of Dubai Marina, the marine club next door, views of the Palm, this hotel has a lot going for it.

One&Only Royal Mirage
Al Sufouh; tel: 04 399 9999; www.oneandonlyroyalmirage.com; $$$
One of Dubai's most romantic places to stay, this gorgeous, Moroccan-styled resort sprawls along the beach for the best part of a kilometre. The resort features three separate hotels, fabulous décor, thousands of palm trees, superb restaurants and the fashionable Kasbar nightclub.

One&Only Royal Mirage poolside area

The Ritz-Carlton Dubai

Dubai Marina; tel: 04 399 4000;
www.ritzcarlton.com; $$$

A little bit of Andalusia in the Gulf, the low-standing, hacienda-style Ritz-Carlton has 138 rooms, all of which are sea-facing. More than many other hotels on the coast, it's a quiet retreat for rest and relaxation, far removed from the crowds of larger beach resorts.

Rixos The Palm

Palm Jumeirah; tel: 04 457 5555;
http://thepalmdubai.rixos.com; $$$

With a long curving beach around the end of the outer breakwater, the Rixos has great views of the Dubai coastline and the rest of the Palm. Inside it is stylish and relatively simple, without any unnecessary frills; outside, the gardens are thick with palm trees, shaded sunbeds and three swimming pools.

Further out

Al Maha Resort

Dubai–Al Ain Road (E66); tel: 04 832 9900;
www.al-maha.com; $$$$

Meaning 'gazelle' in Arabic, Al Maha offers the most Arabian accommodation in Dubai without any compromise on luxury. Not so much a hotel as a Bedu desert encampment of 30 luxury chalet 'tents' within the Dubai Desert Conservation Reserve (see page 69), this is Dubai's first eco-tourism resort. Activities include camel riding, falconry displays and desert safaris.

Bab Al Shams Desert Resort & Spa

Endurance City; tel: 04 809 6100;
www.meydanhotels.com; $$$

Located in the desert near Endurance City some 37km (23 miles) from Arabian Ranches, Bab Al Shams ('Gate of the Sun') is popular with city residents as a weekend getaway and it is a good – and cheaper – alternative to Al Maha Resort.

Desert Palm PER AQUUM

Al Awir Road, nr Intl City; tel: 04 323 8888;
www.minorhotels.com; $$$

For a break away from the buzzing city, this low-key resort offers accommodation on the outskirts of Dubai in villas looking out over the fields of the 160-acre polo club, with some top-class dining options.

Jebel Ali Beach Hotel

Jebel Ali, south of Dubai city; tel: 04 814 5555; www.jaresortshotels.com; $$$

Located just south of the city, this resort seems like a world away from Dubai, and is all the better for it. With views out to sea without a high-rise in sight, the hotel and landscaped gardens are well established, and the perfect place to unwind.

Kempinski Hotel Mall of the Emirates

Mall of the Emirates, Al Barsha; tel: 04 341 0000; www.kempinski.com; $$$

As well as all of the mall to explore, this hotel is well placed for both 'old' and 'new' Dubai, and has the unique Aspen Chalets, where rooms overlook the snowy slopes of Ski Dubai.

Al Dawaar revolving restaurant

RESTAURANTS

You won't go hungry in Dubai – quite the opposite in fact, as the city continues to consolidate its position as the food capital of the Middle East. As you would expect, the city is a particularly good place to sample Arabian cuisine, but at the culinary crossroads between Europe, Asia and Arabia, it offers a cosmopolitan spread of cuisines, in a huge variety of settings. At the bottom of the scale, you can eat well for just a handful of dirhams at one of the city's streetside shwarma stands, inexpensive Lebanese cafés, or in one of the hundreds of bargain-basement curry houses that can be found throughout Bur Dubai and Karama. At the top of the scale, the sky's the limit, with opulent restaurants in spectacular waterfront or high-rise locations.

If you want to drink alcohol with your meal, your eating options are immediately restricted to licensed restaurants in hotels – although don't assume that just because a place is unlicensed the food will be below par. Wherever you're going, the best places can get booked up quickly, particularly at weekends; so it pays to reserve.

There's a vast range of different places to eat in the city's myriad hotels, ranging from functional 24-hour coffee shops and buffet restaurants through to ultra-swanky fine-dining palaces. The majority of hotel restaurants are licensed, although there are exceptions. Many of the best places take advantage of their spectacular locations. These include a number of magical beachfront restaurants, plus various places in spectacular high-rise locations at (or near) the top of the city's skyscrapers. Other places take advantage of waterside locations around the city.

For something with a more local flavour, Dubai's hotels are a good place to sample traditional Arabian fare, often with live music and belly-dancing – these places frequently don't get going till late, but stay lively into the small hours.

The Dubai Friday brunch is a city institution, equivalent to the British Sunday roast. It's particularly popular amongst the city's Western expat set, while many restaurants – especially the hotel venues – lay on all-you-can-eat (and sometimes drink, as well) deals. Brunch usually kicks off around midday, and can last for the remainder of the afternoon.

Price guide for a two-course meal for two, with a glass of wine each where alcohol is available:
$$$$$ = over Dhs500
$$$$ = Dhs400–500
$$$ = Dhs200–400
$$ = Dhs100–200
$ = below Dhs100

Smart style at Table 9

Bur Dubai and Karama

Bastakiah Nights

Al Fahidi Historical Neighbourhood, Dubai; tel: 04 353 7772; daily 12.30–11.30pm; $$$

Located in an historic courtyard house in the 'Bastakiya' district, this is one of the city's most atmospheric and romantic restaurants. The menu features a mix of Arabian and Iranian dishes. No alcohol. Dress: smart casual.

Chhappan Bhog

Trade Centre Road, Karama; tel: 04 396 8176; daily 9am–11pm; $$

The North Indian vegetarian meals served here are so delicious that they will please the taste buds of even the most die-hard meat eaters. No alcohol. Dress: casual.

Deira

Al Dawaar

Hyatt Regency Hotel, Deira; tel: 04 209 1234; www.dubai.regency.hyatt.com; daily 12.30–3.30pm and 6.30pm–midnight; $$$–$$$$

On the 25th floor of the Hyatt Regency, Dubai's only revolving restaurant boasts stunning views of Deira and Bur Dubai complemented by an upmarket (if rather expensive) international buffet. Alcohol. Dress: smart casual.

Ashiana by Vineet

Sheraton Dubai Creek, Baniyas Rd; tel: 04 207 1733; www.ashianadubai.com; Sun–Thu noon–3pm & 7.00–11.00pm; Fri & Sat 7.00–11.00pm; $$$–$$$$

One of Dubai's oldest, but now revamped and under the control of Michelin-starred Vineet Bhatia, it specialises in hearty Indian cuisine served up in rich and flavoursome sauces. Alcohol. Dress: smart casual.

Shabestan

Radisson Blu, Dubai Deira Creek, Baniyas Rd; tel: 04 222 7171; www.radissonblu.com daily 12.30–3.15pm and 7.30–11pm; $$$–$$$$

Arguably the best Iranian restaurant in the city, specialising in huge *chelo* kebabs, fish stews and other Persian specialities, served up to the accompaniment of the resident Iranian band playing a violin, drum and *santour* (nightly except Saturday). Alcohol. Dress: smart casual.

Table 9

Hilton Dubai Creek, Baniyas Road; tel: 04 212 7551; www.table9dubai.com; Sun–Fri 6.30pm–11pm; $$$$

Formerly Gordon Ramsay's Verre, this outstanding restaurant was taken over by chef Darren Velvick in 2014. It offers the same top-notch modern European fine-dining as before, but with a more flexible menu, relaxed ambience and lower prices. Alcohol. Dress: smart casual.

Al Garhoud

Blue Elephant

Al Bustan Rotana Hotel, Garhoud; tel: 04

Al Nafoorah

282 0000; www.blueelephant.com/dubai; Mon–Sat noon–3.30pm and 7–midnight, closed Tue night; $$$

Always a candidate for best Thai restaurant in Dubai, located in a quaint Thai-style village setting in the Rotana hotel. Alcohol. Dress: smart casual.

Reflets Par Pierre Gagnaire

InterContinental Dubai, Festival City; tel: 04 701 1127; www.diningdfc.com; daily 7pm–late; $$$$$

Arguably Dubai's top restaurant, showcasing Pierre Gagnaire's innovative contemporary French cooking, served with enormous panache. Alcohol. Dress: smart.

The Thai Kitchen

Park Hyatt, Port Saeed; tel: 04 602 1814, www.dubai.park.hyatt.com; daily 7pm–midnight, also Friday brunch 12.30–4pm; $$$$

One of the best and most romantic Thai restaurants in town, set on the Park Hyatt's idyllic creek-side terrace and offering a sumptuous range of unusual regional specialities. Alcohol. Dress: smart casual.

Oud Metha and Umm Hurair

Asha's

Wafi Mall; tel: 04 324 4100; www.ashasrestaurants.com; daily 12.30–3pm and 7.00–midnight; $$$–$$$$.

Owned by legendary Bollywood chanteuse Asha Bhosle, this restaurant offers a good range of Indian classics alongside more unusual regional specialities, including recipes from Asha's own cookbook. There's another branch in Mall of The Emirates. Alcohol.

Khazana

Al Nasr Leisureland, Oud Metha; tel: 04 336 0061; http://khanakhazanadubai.net; daily 12.30–3pm, 7–11.30pm; $$$

Owned by Indian celebrity chef Sanjeev Kapoor, Khazana does excellent North Indian specialities in a village-style conservatory setting. Alcohol. Dress: smart casual.

Medzo

Pyramids Wafi, Umm Hurair; tel: 04 324 4100; daily 7.30–11.30pm, Friday lunch 12.30–3pm; $$$

A suave little restaurant offering top-notch Italian cuisine in a stylish but laid-back setting. Alcohol.

Sheikh Zayed Road

Al Nafoorah

Emirates Towers, Sheikh Zayed Road; tel: 04 319 8760; www.jumeirah.com; daily 12.00–3.30pm and 7pm–11.30am; $$$

One of the top Lebanese restaurants in town, with a great-value lunch menu and pleasant terrace. Look out for Sheikh Mohammed, who is purported to drop in from time to time. Alcohol. Dress: smart casual.

Alta Badia

Emirates Towers Hotel, Sheikh Zayed Road; tel: 04 319 8771; www.jumeirah.com; daily

Dish at The Thai Kitchen

12–3pm, 6pm–midnight, closed Fri lunch; $$$$$
The views from the 50th floor of the landmark Emirates Towers hotel are stunning, but the food in this new Italian is also top notch. The Alta Badia bar, upstairs, is a fine place for a pre- or post-dinner drinks. Alcohol. Dress: smart.

Après

Mall of the Emirates; tel: 04 341 2575; daily 12am–midnight; $$$
Chic bar and restaurant overlooking the snowy slopes of Ski Dubai and offering a good range of international fare – anything from coq au vin to fish and chips – backed up by one of the city's best cocktail lists. Alcohol. Dress: smart casual.

At.mosphere

Burj Khalifa, Downtown Dubai; tel: 04 888 3828, www.atmosphereburjkhalifa.com. $$$$$
At.mosphere is the world's highest bar and restaurant, located on the 122nd floor of the soaring Burj Khalifa, the world's tallest building. Choose between the lounge for a drink, light meal or pricey afternoon tea and the restaurant, offering upmarket fare in its elegant dining room. Alcohol. Dress: smart.

The Exchange Grill

Fairmont Hotel, Sheikh Zayed Road; tel: 04 311 8316, www.fairmont.com/dubai; daily 7pm–midnight; $$$$$
An exclusive steakhouse, and one of Dubai's best, this small and very upmarket establishment serves up choice gold Angus and Wagyu cuts, backed up by one of the city's most extensive wine lists. Dress: smart casual.

More Cafe

Mall of the Emirates; www.morecafe.co; daily 8am–11.30pm; $$
A funky Dutch-owned bistro with a wide range of superior international café fare. A difficult place to beat for its combination of excellent atmosphere, quality, value and service. Another branch at Al Murooj Complex. No alcohol. Dress: casual.

Trader Vic's

Crowne Plaza, Sheikh Zayed Road; tel: 04 331 1111; www.tradervics.com; daily noon–3pm and 6pm–1.30am; $$$$
A happy mishmash of styles – Polynesia meets Asia and the Caribbean – this upbeat bar and restaurant has live music, a party atmosphere, and is popular for cocktails in Happy Hour. A second branch is at Souk Madinat Jumeirah, with a Mai-Tai Lounge at Al Fattan Towers in Dubai Marina. Alcohol. Dress: smart casual.

Zuma

The Gate Village 06, DIFC; tel: 04 425 5660, www.zumarestaurant.com; Sat–Thu 12–3pm, Fri/Sat 12.30–4pm, plus daily 7pm–midnight (Thu–Fri until 1am); $$$$

Al Mahara: dine by a giant aquarium

This über-chic bar-restaurant is a hit with Dubai's fashionistas, local foodies and the local business lunch set, thanks to its cool ambience and excellent range of classic and contemporary Japanese fare. Alcohol. Dress: smart.

Jumeira and Umm Suqeim

Al Mahara

Burj Al Arab, Umm Suqeim; tel: 04 301 7600; www.burj-al-arab.com; daily 12.30–3pm and 7pm–midnight; $$$$$
Centred around an enormous fish tank, this spectacularly designed subterranean seafood restaurant is one of Dubai's most expensive, with sumptuous international seafood. Alcohol. Dress: smart.

Al Qasr

Dubai Marine Beach Resort & Spa, Jumeira Road; tel: 04 346 1111; www.dxbmarine.com; daily 12.30–3.30pm and 7pm–2am; $$$$
An upmarket Lebanese restaurant with a wide-ranging menu of mezze and grills, plus shisha and live music with belly dancing later in the evening. Alcohol. Dress: smart casual.

Almaz by Momo

Harvey Nichols, Mall of the Emirates; tel: 04 409 8877; daily 10am–midnight; $$$
Dubai version of the celebrity hangout in London, offering mezze and traditional Moroccan mains in a trendy, contemporary North African-themed interior. A second branch is now open in The Beach at Dubai Marina with views of the sea and the Dubai Eye. No alcohol. Dress: smart casual.

Amala

Jumeirah Zabeel Saray, The Palm Jumeirah, tel: 04 453 0444; daily 6pm–1am, weekends also lunch 1–4pm; $$$$
Indian fine-dining restaurant in the new Jumeirah Zabeel Saray hotel, this place has had rave reviews for its opulent décor and superb classical North Indian cooking – and the tasting menu at Dhs325 is a good deal. Alcohol. Dress: smart casual.

Automatic

Jumeira Road and JBR, Dubai Marina; www.automaticrestaurant.com; daily 8am–late; $
Chain of budget Lebanese restaurants offering good mezze and grills at very affordable prices. No alcohol. Dress: casual.

Beachcombers

Jumeirah Beach Hotel, Umm Suqeim; tel: 04 432 3232; www.jumeirah.com; daily 12.30–4pm and 6.30–11.30pm; $$$
This Southeast Asian restaurant with a thatched terrace overlooking the spectacular Burj Al Arab is difficult to beat for its views. There's an à-la-carte menu for lunch and buffet for dinner. Families are welcome. Alcohol. Dress: smart casual.

Japengo

Mall of the Emirates, Sheikh Zayed Road, tel: 04 341 1671; daily 11–1am, until midnight Sun–Thu, until 1am Fri; $$

Amala's Indian cuisine

Chic café-restaurant, with an eclectic menu featuring everything from sushi and sashimi through to stir-fries, pizzas, pastas, mezze and lamb chops, plus sandwiches and salads. There are other branches, including one overlooking the canal in the Souk Madinat Jumeirah, the other in Mirdif City Centre and the DIFC district. No alcohol. Dress: casual.

Pai Tai
Al Qasr Hotel, Madinat Jumeirah; tel: 04 366 6730; www.jumeirah.com; daily 6.30–11.30pm plus Fri/Sat 12.30am–2.45pm; $$$$

This is one of the city's most romantic places to eat, with live music and stunning Burj Al Arab views from the candlelit terrace. The menu features all the usual Thai classics, including spicy salads, and meat and seafood curries. Alcohol. Dress: smart casual.

Pierchic
Al Qasr Hotel, Madinat Jumeirah; tel: 04 432 3232; www.jumeirah.com; daily 12–3pm (except Fri for brunch) and 6.30–11.30pm; $$$$$

So romantic, and oh so chic, this international seafood restaurant at the end of its own wooden pier offers stunning views of Burj Al Arab and the Madinat Jumeirah resort. Alcohol. Dress: smart.

Sho Cho
Dubai Marine Beach Resort, Jumeira; tel: 04 346 1111; www.dxbmarine.com; daily 7pm–3am; $$$

This fashionable hang out for Dubai's beautiful people overlooks a small beach and is part sushi restaurant and part cocktail bar and nightclub. Alcohol. Dress: smart casual.

Zheng He's
Mina A'Salam, Madinat Jumeirah; tel: 04 366 6730; www.jumeirah.com; daily noon–3pm and 7–11.30pm; $$$$

One of the top Chinese restaurants in Dubai, with sumptuous décor and superb classic and contemporary fare. Alcohol. Dress: smart casual.

Dubai Marina

Indego by Vineet
Grosvenor House Hotel; tel: 04 317 6000; www.indegobyvineet.com; daily 7pm–midnight; $$$$

Overseen by Vineet Bhatia, India's first Michelin-starred chef, this stylish restaurant showcases Bhatia's outstanding contemporary Indian cooking, with a seductive blend of sub-continental and international ingredients and techniques. Alcohol. Dress: smart casual.

Rhodes W1
Grosvenor House Hotel; tel: 04 317 6000; www.rw1-dubai.com; Mon–Sat 7–11.30pm, Fri/Sat 2.30–5pm; $$$$$

Dubai outpost of UK celebrity chef Gary Rhodes, with an inventive menu showcasing Rhodes' distinctive brand of modern European cuisine, accompanied by classic British deserts like bread and butter pudding. Alcohol. Dress: smart casual.

NIGHTLIFE

Nightlife in Dubai is a mix of the traditional and the contemporary. For many local Emiratis, after-dark activity consists largely of sitting back over endless cups of coffee, shooting the breeze and watching the world go by while puffing away on a shisha (waterpipe) – a lot easier on the nose than your average smoke-fogged pub. Elements (see page 47) in Wafi, Kan Zaman in Bur Dubai (see page 34), and Shakespeare & Co. on Sheikh Zayed Road (see page 54) are three good places to try. Many parts of the old city also come alive at night, particularly in Deira and Bur Dubai – when the neon comes on and the souks fill up with shoppers, ranging from local expat Indians and Pakistanis through to European tourists, Russian bargain-hunters and West African gold traders – and in Satwa and Karama.

In terms of more contemporary entertainment, the city boasts a superb selection of bars and a reasonable club scene, kept going by a flow of eager tourists, Western expats and the city's smart Lebanese party set. Cultural attractions are relatively thin on the ground, unless your visit coincides with a major event like Art Dubai, or the jazz and film festivals.

Clubs in Dubai come, go and change name and DJ on a regular basis. Check out the latest listings in *Time Out Dubai* (www.timeoutdubai.com), What's On (http://whatson.ae), ShortList (www.shortlistdubai.com) or visit www.platinumlist.ae to find out where's new and hot.

Entrance charges at clubs vary wildly Dhs50–100 is more usual, while prices might be even higher if there's a big-name DJ lined up. Most places also have a couples-only policy and heavy-duty doormen. At sniffier venues you'll also need to dress to impress, or expect to be turned away.

Ladies Nights are a Dubai institution. These are usually held on Wednesday, or, most commonly, Tuesday nights in an attempt to drum up custom during the quieter midweek evenings, with lots of places around the city offering all sorts of deals for girls, ranging from a couple of free cocktails up to complimentary champagne all night. Pick up a copy of *Time Out Dubai* (or check www.timeoutdubai.com) or *What's On* for listings.

Bars

360°

Jumeirah Beach Hotel; tel: 04 406 8741; www.jumeirah.com; nightly from 5pm–late; occasional entrance charges

Principally a bar, although also hosts local and visiting DJs. Whatever's on offer, this is one of the city's finest chill-out spaces, overlooking the coast, JBH and Burj Al Arab from the end of a long breakwater – a great place to relax over a beer or shisha.

Alta Badia Bar

Jumeirah Emirates Towers Hotel, Trade Centre; tel: 04 432 3232; www.jumeirah. com; daily 6pm–1.30am

One of the loftiest licensed venues in Dubai, on the 51st floor of the Emirates Towers hotel building, with futuristic décor and huge views out through the wall to ceiling windows. Also boasts one of the city's biggest drinks lists, and pre-dinner Happy Hour sundowners including 50 percent off some drinks and cocktails daily from 6-9pm.

Barasti Bar

Le Meridien Mina Seyahi, Al Sufouh; tel: 04 399 3333; www.barastibeach. com; Sat–Wed 11am–1.30am, Thu–Fri 11am–3am

Low-key, friendly and relaxed, the Barasti Bar is opposite of the glitz and pomposity of some of Dubai's nightpots. Free entry lets you use the beach and facilities, while evenings see sport on big screens, happy hour drinks, good bar food and some of Dubai's best parties, all on the beach.

Buddha Bar

Grosvenor House, Dubai Marina; tel: 04 317 6000; www.buddhabar-dubai.com; Sat–Wed 7.30pm–2am, Thu–Fri 7.30pm–3am

Dubai's branch of the Paris-based chain, this bar still creates a wow with the impressive interior, and Pan-Asian food. Early evening it tends to attract diners, later on things really start to get going, sound tracked by the Buddha Bar's trademark mix of chilled grooves and their signature cocktails.

Irish Village

Dubai Tennis Stadium, Al Garhoud; tel: 04 282 4750; www.theirishvillage.com; Sat–Wed 11.30am–1am, Thu–Fri 11.30am–2am

Located in 'Old Dubai', and still popular, the Irish Village offers real Irish pub flavour, cosy interior, a large terrace with a lawn and a pond complete with ducks, decent food, good beers, including Guinness, and great craic.

Sho Cho

Dubai Marine Beach Resort, Jumeira; tel: 04 346 1111; www.dxbmarine.com; daily 7.30pm–2am or later

The sea-facing terrace bar at this small Japanese restaurant remains one of the prime places to pose in town, attracting a mix of tourists and beautiful people from the local Lebanese party set. The resident DJ (Sun and Wed–Fri) provides a suitably mellow chill-out soundtrack.

Skyview Bar

Burj Al Arab, Umm Suqeim; tel: 04 301 7600; www.jumeirah.com; Sat–Thu 1pm–2am, Fri 7pm–2am

Landmark bar almost at the top of the Burj Al Arab, with psychedelic décor and vast sea and city views. The drinks menu is particularly strong on cocktails (from Dhs100), but you'll need to reserve in advance and there's a minimum spend of Dhs350 per person, or

Concert at Dubai Media City Amphitheatre

to see the views in daylight, the afternoon tea runs from 1–5pm.

Clubs

Boudoir

Dubai Marine Beach Resort, Jumeira; tel: 04 345 5995; www.dxbmarine.com; nightly 9pm–3am

This over-the-top bar-cum-nightclub attracts some the city's most showy residents, who come to strut about the club's decadent interior (looking like a kind of plush, 19th-century Parisian brothel) whilst consuming indecent quantities of champagne. Music includes a mix of hip hop and house, with occasional visiting international DJs.

Kasbar

The Palace, One&Only Royal Mirage, Al Sufouh; tel: 04 399 3999; www. oneandonlyresorts.com; Mon–Sat 9.30pm–3am

Catering to an older and relatively sedate crowd (over 25s only), this upmarket club shares the opulent Moroccan styling of the rest of the Royal Mirage complex. Music is usually a mix of Arabian and international tunes. It gets lively at times, but if things are slow it's worth checking out the nearby Rooftop Bar, which also has live music most evenings.

Pacha Ibiza Dubai

Souk Madinat Jumeirah; tel: 04 567 0000; http://pacha.ae; Tue–Sat 8pm–3am

Previously the home to superclub Trilogy, this latest addition to Dubai's club circuit from international brand Pacha has separate areas offering different music – including on the rooftop – plus a supper club with extravagant entertainment, and brings with it a lot of style from the white isle, making it still one of Dubai's top nightclubs.

White Dubai

Meydan Racecourse, Nad Al Sheba; tel: 050 443 0933; www.whitedubai.com; Thu–Sat 11pm–3am

For the ultimate nightclub experience in Dubai, try this venture on the top of the Meydan grandstand for Beirut's top club event. White Dubai sees the bar raised in terms of exclusivity, the show on offer, and the queues trying to get in! Making a reservation will help cut entry times down, and once inside, the cutting edge house and EDM comes courtesy from top resident DJs and visiting international DJs and stars.

Zinc

Crowne Plaza Hotel, Trade Centre; tel: 04 331 1111; www.myspace.com/zincdubai; nightly 10pm–3am

One of the longest running clubs in Dubai, known for its relaxed atmosphere, eclectic soundtrack and general reputation for unpretentious partying. Music features a mix of retro, R&B, hip hop and house depending on the night.

Madinat Theatre

Live music

Dubai Media City Amphitheatre
Dubai Media city; tel: 04 391 1111
Increasing numbers of well-known international rock and pop acts are visiting Dubai. Concerts are usually held at the Dubai Media City Amphitheatre, with a capacity of 15,000 (it also hosts the annual Dubai Jazz Festival). Check *Time Out Dubai* (www.timeoutdubai. com) and What's On (http://whatson. ae) for upcoming gigs.

Malecon
Dubai Marine Beach Resort, Jumeira; tel: 04 346 1111; www.dxbmarine.com; nightly 6.30pm–late
A colourful Cuban bar, restaurant and club rolled into one, with walls covered in graffiti and live Latin bands during the night; 9am–11am (except Sat, when there are salsa classes at 10pm), followed by a DJ.

Peanut Butter Jam
Wafi, Oud Metha; tel: 04 324 4100; www.pyramidsrestaurantsatwafi.com; Fri from Oct–May 7.30pm–midnight
Laidback music evenings held on the open-air rooftop terrace of the Wafi complex. Sink into a giant beanbag under the stars and listen to local jazz musicians and pop bands performing a mix of cover versions and assorted original tunes.

Performing arts

Dubai Community and Arts Centre (DUCTAC)
Mall of the Emirates, Sheikh Zayed Road; tel: 04 341 4777; www.ductac.org
One of the few places in the city keeping the cultural flicker alight, DUCTAC is home to a trio of lively little venues: the Centrepoint Theatre, Kilachand Studio Theatre and Manu Chhabria Arts Centre, which host a wide range of productions, including film, dance, music and theatre (several shows aimed at children), with the emphasis on local and community-based projects.

Dubai Opera
Downtown Dubai; http://dubaiopera.com
Located in one of Dubai's new iconic buildings in The Opera District, the Dubai Opera opened in 2016, providing a word-class venue for concerts, theatre, ballet and shows, in a top quality venue that changes for the type of event it is hosting. Opening night was in August 2016, with Plácido Domingo, and the first calendar year's calendar was packed with big name stars and operas and shows. Check the website for details of what's on.

Madinat Theatre
Madinat Jumeirah; tel: 04 366 6546; www.madinattheatre.com
Dubai's first proper theatre when it opened in the mid-noughties, although don't expect much beyond a fairly predictable range of mainstream musicals, children's shows and other crowd-pleasers.

Dubai Marina in the mist

A–Z

A

Age restrictions

Car rental agencies require drivers to be at least 21 or 22 years old. This rises to 25 and 30 depending on the vehicle category. Children under 10 are not allowed to sit in the front passenger seat of cars. Entry to bars and nightclubs varies between 18 and 21. ID checks are often carried out (even if you look way older). On the water and in theme parks, the minimum age for some activities is seven or eight, but it also depends on the height of the child (often with a minimum of 1.2m/4ft). For diving lessons, the minimum age for junior open water training is 10, but kids can begin learning in a pool from the age of eight.

Alcohol

Unless you're a Dubai resident with an alcohol licence, you may only buy alcohol for consumption in hotel bars, restaurants and clubs, and in a very small number of mall restaurants. Drinking alcohol in public, outside licensed venues, is strictly illegal.

B

Budgeting for your trip

Dubai is an expensive city to visit. Accommodation is probably the main expense, while fancier restaurants and alcohol all come at a considerable price. On the plus side, it's also possible to eat well and very cheaply at many places around the city, while public transport, either on the city's metro or in taxis, is also good value for money.

Accommodation: The cost for a standard double room ranges from around Dhs350 per night in a one-star city centre hotel to Dhs575–1,000 at a four-star hotel, and Dhs1,000–3,500 at a five-star hotel.

Eating and drinking: It is possible to pick up a filling sandwich in a street-level Lebanese restaurant or a curry (or *thali* set meal) in a no-nonsense Indian or Pakistani outlet for as little as Dhs15. Main courses in most decent Western-style, non-hotel restaurants are between Dhs25–45. For fine dining, budget upwards of Dhs55 per person for mains. For a three-course dinner for two with wine at a five-star hotel venue, budget for upwards of Dhs600.

Cans of soft drinks start at Dhs1 in shops, but are heavily marked up in restaurants. Freshly made juices cost between Dhs6–25. Alcoholic drinks are generally more expensive than they would be in the West.

Transport: Package deals arranged from your home country are likely to be cheaper than separately arranged air travel and accommodation. The best

Jumeirah's beach park

prices are found in low season (July–September), but that's because it is the hottest time of the year in the UAE (and may be only for the hardcore sun fans).

Generally taxis are cheaper than those in Western cities, although the taxi fare from the airport comes with a Dhs20 mark-up. A creek crossing on an *abra* (water taxi) is just Dhs1, while fares on the city's metro and buses are also just a few dirhams.

Bargaining

Don't assume that because of Dubai's tax-free reputation, everything here is cheaper than elsewhere in the world. You can bargain for deals in the souks, but not in malls, except perhaps when buying carpets or large souvenirs, and you are more likely to get a large discount with cash. The trick is to disguise your interest in the item you really want, then offer half of what you're prepared to pay, and take it from there.

Children

Childcare facilities are on a par with those in the West. Most malls have changing facilities in the women's public toilets; many also have supervised indoor play areas.

Climate

Summers are very hot and humid. From May to September, daytime temperatures rarely fall below 40°C (104°F) with humidity up to 90 per cent. From October to April the weather resembles that of an exceptionally good European summer, with temperatures hovering around 30°C (mid-80s°F) and little or no humidity.

Evenings can feel a little chilly around January and February, so jumpers may be required. Annual rainfall is minimal (an average of 42mm/1.5in), but downpours occur from January to March – and when it rains, it pours. Inland, the desert and mountains are a little cooler (especially up a height), and particularly at night in winter.

Clothing

Comfortable loose cottons suit the climate best, with peak caps or sun hats for optimum protection during the heat of the day. In terms of culture, while the most daring swimwear is acceptable on the beach, around town visitors should be more modest and avoid wearing very short shorts and dresses, and tight tops. Outside Dubai, more care should be taken to avoid showing too much bare skin: upper arms should be covered, and women are advised to wear long skirts or trousers. Winter evenings can be surprisingly cool, so pack a cardigan or jumper.

Crime and safety

Dubai is a relatively safe city. Both petty theft and major crimes are rare and the level of personal security is high. Many women feel comfortable on their own

in the evening. However, while you can let your guard down to some extent, it is best to avoid complacency; take the same precautions you would take anywhere else.

Tourists typically find themselves in trouble with the law because they are unaware of, or have disregarded UAE laws regarding alcohol, drugs and public displays of affection. Drunken or disorderly behaviour (including swearing) could land you a spell in prison. It is important to note that some medication (such as codeine and temazepam), available over the counter in other parts of the world, are illegal in the UAE. Check with your health practitioner before entering the country. The UAE also practises zero tolerance to drugs and drink driving.

The US-led 'war on terror' has caused increased concerns for the safety of citizens of countries associated with military activity in the region. The UAE is no exception and vigilance against terrorism is recommended. However, there have been no incidents to date, the country is an ally of the US, and Emiratis are generally friendly to Westerners.

Dubai Police has a Tourist Security Department, tel: 800 4438.

Customs

The duty-free allowances entering the UAE are as follows: 400 cigarettes, 50 cigars or 0.5kg (1lb) loose tobacco, and – for non-Muslims – four litres of alcohol (or 24 cans of beer). There are no limits on perfume.

Disabled travellers

Dubai is one the Middle East's most accessible destinations. Most of the city's more upmarket hotels now have specially adapted rooms for disabled travellers, as do some of the city's malls, including disabled parking spaces and specially equipped toilets. Transport is also fairly well-equipped. Dubai Taxi (tel: 04 208 0808) has specially designed vehicles equipped with ramps and lifts, while the Dubai Metro features tactile guide paths, lifts and ramps to assist visually- and mobility-impaired visitors, as well as wheelchair spaces in all compartments. The city's water buses can also be used by mobility-impaired visitors, and staff will assist you in boarding and disembarking. There are also dedicated facilities for passengers with special needs at the airport. Sadly, most of the city's older heritage buildings are not accessible (with the exception of the Dubai Museum).

Electricity

Voltage in Dubai is 220/240 volts, 50 cycles AC. British-style three-pin sockets are common; if needed, adaptors can be bought from electrical shops all over the city.

Water traffic in Dubai Creek

Embassies and consulates

Australia: BurJuman Centre; tel: 04 508 7100; http://uae.embassy.gov.au.
Canada: 7th floor, Bank Street Building, Bur Dubai; tel: 04 404 8444; www.canadainternational.gc.ca/uae-eau.
France: API World Tower, Sheikh Zayed Road; tel: 04 408 4900; www.consulfrance-dubai.org.
Ireland: Abu Dhabi; www.dfa.ie/irish-embassy/uae/.
New Zealand: Abu Dhabi; tel: 02 441 1222; www.mfat.govt.nz/en/countries-and-regions/middle-east/dubai/new-zealand-embassy/contactfull.
South Africa: Abu Dhabi; tel: 02 447 3446; www.dirco.gov.za/dubai/
UK: Al Seef Road, Bur Dubai; tel: 04 309 4444; www.gov.uk/government/world/organisations/british-embassy-dubai.
US: Dubai World Trade Centre, Sheikh Zayed Road; tel: 04 309 4000; http://dubai.usconsulate.gov.

Emergencies

The emergency number to call for the police or an ambulance is 999; the fire service is on 997. For Dubai Police's Tourist Security Department, dial 800 4438.

Etiquette

Dubai is one of the more liberal Gulf cities, and nationals are both familiar with and reasonably tolerant of those from other cultures. Even so, any extra effort to respect Arab sensibilities is greatly appreciated.

Do not try and rush things, particularly with officialdom, which likes to take its time even over matters of apparent urgency – patience is a virtue; don't photograph men without first asking their permission and never photograph or even stare at local women; don't offer alcohol to Muslims; don't show the soles of your feet when sitting among locals; don't eat, drink or smoke in public areas during the holy month of Ramadan – the penalties are severe; and never drink and drive – you could end up in jail for a month.

Away from the beach, dress modestly, and if time permits, do graciously accept any hospitality that's offered – a refusal would be considered rude.

In addition to dressing appropriately, when visiting a mosque, before entering you will be required to remove your shoes and enter in your bare feet, as is the custom. You should also remove your shoes at the Cultural Centre.

##

Festivals

January–February: Dubai Shopping Festival (DSF), a month-long, city-wide festival with discounts at participating outlets. The festival also includes heritage and entertainment events, funfairs and pyrotechnic shows daily on the Creek, and the popular Global Village (www.globalvillage.ae) in Dubailand, with colourful pavilions showcasing

Dubai's dramatic skyline

arts and crafts from countries around the world.

February: The three-day Dubai International Jazz Festival is held at an open-air venue at Dubai Media City. It regularly attracts some of the best jazz performers in the world. (www.dubai-jazzfest.com).

July–August: A summer version of DSF, the Dubai Summer Surprises (DSS) is another retail happening with most events tending to be held in malls. (www.mydsf.com).

November: The Dubai Airshow is a biennial extravaganza of a trade event that is closed to the public. From the streets around Dubai International Airport, however, you can see afternoon flying displays, such as those by formation team, the Red Arrows. The gala dinner is invitation-only, but the post-dinner concert by a big-name international star is open to the public. For more details, see www.dubaiairshow.org.

December: National Day is a three-day holiday in the first week of December that marks the founding of the UAE in 1971. Parks and public places host cultural activities such as folk dancing, and at night the city is festooned in lights.

The Dubai International Film Festival (DIFF), which was inaugurated in 2004, attracts film-makers and stars from Hollywood, Bollywood and the Middle East. The red-carpet events and most screenings, which members of the public can buy tickets for, are held at Madinat Jumeirah. (www.dubaifilmfest.com).

Gay and lesbian travellers

Homosexuality is not tolerated in the UAE and is officially illegal, so discretion is strongly advised.

Health

Hygien and general health: Dubai is a modern, reasonably clean city. Its public lavatories are well maintained (the WCs are almost all Western-style), and it is safe to drink the tap water, though most residents prefer to drink bottled water, which is advisable anyway outside of Dubai. One of the most popular brands of bottled water is the locally produced Masafi.

Due to widespread construction work, the air in Dubai is very dusty, so people who battle with asthma or their sinuses might suffer.

Medical and dental services: Healthcare is of a high standard in Dubai, but expensive, so it is wise to take out travel insurance. There are good government hospitals as well as numerous private clinics. The main emergency hospital is the government-run Rashid Hospital (tel: 04 337 4000) near Maktoum Bridge in Bur Dubai; emergency treatment is free here. A consultation with a doctor in

Racing camels from above

non-emergency cases costs around Dhs100.

For emergencies with children, Al Wasl Hospital (tel: 04 324 1111), across the highway from Wafi City, is a renowned paediatric hospital.

Dental problems can be dealt with by the American Dental Clinic (tel: 800 83384, http://americandentalclinic. com).

Pharmacies: There are useful branches of the BinSina chain (some open 24 hours), at various locations around the city including at the Mall of The Emirates; Dubai Mall; Mankhool Road in Bur Dubai just north of the Ramada hotel; on the Creek side of Baniyas Square (just east of the Deira Tower); in southern Jumeirah by the turn-off to the Majlis Ghorfat Um Al Sheif; and in Satwa on 2nd December Street near Al Mallah restaurant.

Vaccinations: No special inoculations are required prior to visiting the UAE.

Hours and holidays

Business hours: Dubai runs on an Islamic calendar, with the weekend falling on Friday and Saturday. Government offices work from 7 or 7.30am–1.30pm Sun–Thu. International companies keep the hours of 9am–5pm Sun–Thur, although many work longer hours than in their home countries. Local companies and shops typically open 9/10am– 1/1.30pm and 4/4.30–9/10pm Sat–Thu; some shops in more touristy areas might also stay open throughout the afternoon. Generally, banks are open 8am–1pm Sat–Thu; some also open Fri 8am–noon. Larger shopping malls open from 10am–10pm Sat–Thu and on Fri from around 2pm–late evening.

Public holidays: Religious holidays are governed by the Islamic (Hegira) calendar and therefore do not fall on fixed dates. The main holidays are as follows: Eid Al Fitr (the end of Ramadan); Eid Al Adha (during the month of the Haj, or pilgrimage to Mecca); the ascension of the Prophet; the Prophet's birthday; and Islamic New Year. Check with the Ministry of Information and Culture (www. uaeinteract.com) for dates. Other public holidays are New Year's Day (1 January) and National Day (2 December).

Insurance

Visitors should take out the standard policies that cover loss of property and emergency medical care.

Internet

Access to certain websites may be blocked due to political, religious or sexual content. Internet connectivity is available in the guest rooms and business centres of larger hotels, although often at exorbitant rates. Internet cafés are surprisingly thin on the ground except for in Bur Dubai (where they can be found in many of the small roads and alleyways off Al Fahidi Street).

Things are a lot easier if you have your own WiFi-enabled laptop and can access one of the numerous free WiFi hotspots around the city, which include the whole of the Dubai Mall; a plan is in place to bring WiFi to many of Dubai's beaches. You can also get online on the Dubai Metro for Dhs10 hr. Various WiFi hotspots are also operated by the city's two telecom companies, Eitsalat (www.etisalat.ae) and Du (www.du.ae), which offer access at numerous places around the city, including most of the city's malls and numerous coffee shops, with various pay-as-you-go packages. See the websites for full details of charges and hotspot locations.

L

Language

The official language is Arabic, but English is widely spoken and understood. It's unlikely that you'll encounter any difficulty using English in hotels, restaurants and shopping malls, but it could be useful to learn a few words and phrases in Arabic (see page 132).

Left luggage

The left luggage facility at Dubai International Airport is located in Arrivals (Terminal 1 or 3). At time of printing the cost for a normal size case was Dhs20 for 12 hours. Other options for left luggage are limited to the hotel you have been staying in, which should be willing to hold your luggage for a few hours after you have checked out.

Lost property

There are many stories of lost property being returned. The key is to follow up with the relevant authority or organisation in the general area where your property may have been lost. This might include a local police station, mall management office, taxi company, hotel or bar. It's always worth putting in a call. The number for lost property (Baggage Services) at Dubai International Airport is 04 224 5555 or email them via the lost and found form at www.dubai airports.ae/before-you-fly/baggage/lost-found. If you leave something in a taxi or on the metro, call the RTA on 800 9090.

M

Media

Newspapers: Dubai press is heavily censored and local journalists usually steer well clear of expressing negative or controversial opinions about local matters, making for a rather dull media. International magazines commonly have any offending material (nude women, for example) masked with black marker. Local English-language newspapers are the broadsheet *Gulf News*, *Khaleej Times*, *The Gulf Today*, and the tabloids *Emirates Today* and *7 Days*, although easily the best local paper is *The National*, published in Abu Dhabi,

but with extensive coverage of events in Dubai. Foreign newspapers and English-language publications such as the *International Herald Tribune*, *USA Today* and *Weekly Telegraph* can be found in supermarkets. Most British newspapers arrive a day late, with the exception of *The Times* and *The Sunday Times*, which are printed in Dubai. The main sources of information on events are *Time Out Dubai* and What's On magazines.

Radio: The city has a couple of local English-language radio stations, including Virgin Radio Dubai (104.4 FM; http://virginradiodubai.com) and Dubai 92 (92FM; http://dubai92.com), churning out mainstream western pop and chat.

Television: Dubai's English-language TV station is the government-run Dubai One, which broadcasts Western movies and TV programmes, but has a local English-language news programme, Emirates News, at 8.30pm daily. Hotels also offer satellite and cable television with international news channels such as CNN and Sky.

Money

Cash machines: There are globally linked ATM points at banks, malls and some hotels.

Credit cards: Major cards such as Visa, MasterCard, American Express and Diners Club are widely accepted in hotels, restaurants and shops. But if you plan to bargain, it's better to have cash.

Currency: The UAE dirham (abbreviated to Dhs, dh or AED). One dirham is 100 fils, and, at the time of printing (and since 1980), it was linked to the US dollar at Dhs3.67.

Money changers: More convenient than banks in terms of opening hours and their location in nearly all shopping malls and on the streets in busy shopping areas, money changers also offer better rates than banks. Among them are Al Ansari Exchange (tel: 04 397 7787), Al Fardan Exchange (tel: 04 228 0004), and Thomas Cook Al Rostamani (tel: 04 227 3690). All currencies accepted.

Taxes: A tax and service charge (usually 20 percent) is added to hotel bills. Check this is included in prices quoted.

Tipping: This is not compulsory, and prices in many upmarket hotels and restaurants include a 10 percent service charge. Supermarket employees who pack and carry bags, and petrol pump attendants who clean windscreens, are tipped, but in coins rather than notes.

Travellers' cheques: Easily exchanged at hotels, banks and money changers, travellers' cheques are also sometimes accepted in major shops. Banks are generally open Sat–Thu 8am–1pm only. Money exchanges located in malls and souks keep shop hours.

Photography

Never take photographs of government buildings or military installations. Do not

Persian carpet shop in Sharjah's Central Souk

photograph people (especially women) without asking permission.

Police

Dubai's police force has a low-key, but visible presence across the emirate: its green-and-white BMW and Mercedes patrol cars are a common sight on main highways and in residential neighbourhoods. During rush hour, the traffic flow at busy intersections is typically managed by police motorcyclists.

The emergency number for the police is 999. The toll-free number for general information, including details about the force's new Department for Tourist Security, is 800 4438. The police website is www.dubaipolice.gov.ae. (See also Crime and Safety, page 119.)

Post

Dubai's Central Post Office (Sat–Thu 8am–8pm, Fri 5–9pm) is located on Zabeel Road in Karama. There are smaller post offices around the city, including in Deira (near the Avari Hotel), Satwa (near Ravi's restaurant), Jumeira (on Al Wasl Road), in Bur Dubai on Al Fahidi Street opposite the entrance to Al Fahidi Historical Neighbourhood, and at the international airport.

Sending an airmail letter to Western countries costs around Dhs3–6 and a postcard around Dhs1–2. Allow up to 10 days for delivery. International courier companies operating in Dubai include DHL (tel: 800 4004), FedEx (tel: 800 4050) and UPS (tel: 800 4774).

R

Ramadan rules

Whatever your religion, it is illegal to eat in public in daylight during the holy month of Ramadan, when Muslims abstain from food and drink (and smoke) from sunrise to sunset. Some restaurants open for lunch but screen off their eating areas.

Religion

Islam
Islam is the official religion of the UAE. Nationals are mostly Sunni Muslims.

Christianity
There is freedom of worship for Christians in church compounds on the understanding that they do not proselytise. Christian churches are grouped along Oud Metha Road in Bur Dubai and in Jebel Ali Village. They include Christ Church Jebel Ali (tel: 04 884 5436), the Anglican Holy Trinity (tel: 04 337 0247) and the Roman Catholic St Mary's (tel: 04 337 0087). The main services are held on Friday – the local weekend. Bibles for personal use can be carried into the country.

S

Smoking

In general, the attitude to smoking is similar to that in Western nations. Smoking is banned in all indoor public

Musicians performing at a heritage festival to celebrate Sharjah

venues, including restaurants, malls and offices, although you can still smoke in bars and pubs, in most outdoor eating venues, and in most hotel rooms (although a few hotels are now entirely smoke-free). During Ramadan, smoking in public anywhere is forbidden during daylight hours.

T

Telephones

Direct international telephone dialling is available from all phones. Local calls within Dubai are free from a subscriber's phone. You should not have a problem finding coin- and card-operated public telephones on the streets and in shopping malls. Pre-paid phone cards are available from Etisalat, shops, supermarkets and service stations. Hotels tend to charge a premium for calls. Roaming mobile users will gain access to the local GSM service. As elsewhere, the code for dialling internationally from the UAE is 00 followed by the relevant national code and local number.

Local telecoms provider Etisalat can be contacted by dialling 101 or 144. The number for directory enquiries is 181. Assistance is provided in English and Arabic. Automated answering systems in Dubai tend to begin in Arabic, so hold on for instructions in English.

The international dialling code for the UAE is 971. Dubai's city code is 04 (omit the zero when dialling from overseas). The prefix for mobile numbers in the UAE is 050 or 055 (again, omit the zero when dialling from overseas). US access codes are as follows: AT&T 800121; MCI Worldcom 800111; Sprint 800131.

Time zones

Dubai is GMT (UCT) +4 hours, or BST +3 hours.

Toilets

The majority of places have Western-style toilets, although you may occasionally find squat toilets. Public toilets in busy places (malls etc) are well looked after.

Tourist information

The local Dubai Department of Tourism and Commerce Marketing (DTCM; tel: +971 6005 55559; www.visit dubai.com) is the emirate's official tourism promotion organisation. DTCM's information centres in Dubai include kiosks in Terminals 1 and 3 at Dubai International Airport, and desks in the following malls: Deira City Centre, BurJuman Centre, Wafi City, Mercato and Ibn Battuta. The head office is in the National Bank of Dubai building on the Deira Creekside.

International offices
UK:
4th Floor, 41–46 Nuffield House, Piccadilly, London W1 0DS;

Fishermen pulling in the day's catch on Ajman beach

Tel: 020 7321 6110;
Email: dtcm_uk@dubaitourism.ae
North America:
Tel: +971 4 201 0259
Email: jessica.herring@dubaitourism.ae
Australia & New Zealand:
Tel: +61 2 9956 6620
Email: dtcm_aus@dubaitourism.ae
South Africa:
Tel: +27 11 702 9600;
Email: dtcm_sa@dubaitourism.ae

Tours

Visit www.insightguides.com for tailor-made private trips to Dubai and the UAE.

The leading local tour company is Arabian Adventures, a subsidiary of Emirates airline (tel: 04 303 4888; www.arabian-adventures.com), offering an extensive range of tours. Other reliable operators include Alpha Tours (tel: 04 701 9111, www.alphatours dubai.com), and Orient Tours (tel: 04 282 8238; www.orienttours.ae). All of these companies can arrange desert safaris, dhow cruises and trips to other emirates. For a smaller company offering more personal service and more flexibility of tour itineraries, try Explorer Tours (tel: 04 286 1991; www.explorer tours.ae).

For hot-air ballooning over the desert contact Balloon Adventures Dubai (tel: 04 388 4044; www.ballooning.ae).

The Sheikh Mohammed Centre for Cultural Understanding (tel: 04 353 6666, www.cultures.ae; see page 55) organises tours of Jumeira Mosque, walking tours of Al Fahidi Historical Neighbourhood and cultural lunches.

Transport

Airports and arrival

The main gateway is Dubai International Airport (tel: 04 224 5555; www.dubai-airports.ae), served by many major airlines including Emirates Airlines, British Airways, Virgin Atlantic, Lufthansa, KLM, Air France, Delta, Air India, Singapore Airlines, Malaysia and Thai. Direct flights from the US are provided by Emirates. The flight time to Dubai from Europe is around seven hours; 13 hours from New York.

The airport itself is 10 minutes away from central Deira and a 30- to 45-minute drive from the hotels in the south of the city on the coast. The airport comprises three terminals. The sparkling new terminal 3 is where all Emirates flights arrive/depart; terminal 1 is where most other international flights arrive; while terminal 2 is used by smaller regional carriers. Both terminals 1 and 3 have their own dedicated Metro station, as well as tourist information and car rental desks, ATMs and places to exchange money. Regular airport buses also serve the airport, and there are several taxis, although note that taxis picked up at the airport incur a Dhs25 surcharge. The fare from the airport to Deira and Bur Dubai will be around Dhs30–40; considera-

bly more (upwards of Dhs80) to 'New Dubai' in the south.

There is no airport departure tax on leaving Dubai.

Transport within Dubai

Nol tickets: Almost all public transport in Dubai – metro, buses and waterbuses (but not *abras*) is covered by the Nol integrated ticket system (www.nol.ae). You'll need to get a pre-paid Nol card before you can travel. Cards can be bought (or topped up) at any Metro station, at numerous bus stops, or at branches of Carrefour, Spinneys, Waitrose and Emirates NBD Bank. There are four types of card/ticket. The Red Card has been designed for visitors, costing just Dhs2, although this has to be topped up with the correct fare before each journey and can only be recharged ten times; you might prefer the more flexible Silver Card (Dhs20, including Dhs14 credit), which stores up to Dhs500 of credit and lasts five years.

Dubai Metro: Since opening in 2009, Dubai's state-of-the-art Metro system (http://dubaimetro.eu) has made getting to either end of the city cheaper than before (taxis were often the only option). The system comprises a mix of overground and underground lines, with bright modern stations and automatic driverless trains, although the popularity of the system means that it is often difficult to get a seat. The lines currently open are the Red Line, which runs from Rashidiya via the airport and old city and then down through Karama and along Sheikh Zayed Road all the way to Jebel Ali, at the far southern edge of the city; and the Green Line, which loops around Bur Dubai and Deira, and links into the Red Line at one station on either side of the creek. These two lines will be added to in the future, as well as three new lines to be introduced on different routes.

Trains run approximately every 10 minutes from 5.30am–midnight Sat–Wed, Thu until 1am, and Fri 10am–1am). Fares start at around Dhs2 up to Dhs7 in standard class, or from around Dhs4 to Dhs14 in the superior Gold Class. The Gold cars are worth the extra for great views out of the end of the train, slightly plusher carriages, and are much less packed. Tickets are checked, and you'll get fined if you are in Gold with a normal ticket.

Tram: Introduced in 2014, the Dubai Tram (www.thedubaitram.com) has an 11km (6.8 mile) route around Dubai Marina and Al Sufouh, with 11 stations, that links into the Dubai Metro system, as well as the Palm Jumeirah Monorail system. It is due to expand to service destinations such as Burj Al Arab, Madinat Jumeirah and Mall of the Emirates, with an estimated completion date of 2020. Trams run Sun–Thu 6.30am–1.30am, Fri 9am–1.30am. Fares are paid for using the Nol system (www.nol.ae), and start around Dhs3.

A sand storm in the desert

Taxis: You'll need to catch a cab to places not covered by the Metro or Tram. Cabs are metered, air-conditioned, clean and reliable. The flag-fare is Dhs5–71 (or Dhs25 from the airport). The main operators are Dubai Taxi, Cars Taxi, Metro Taxi and National Taxi. You can book a cab by calling 04 208 0808, but they are usually picked up from stands at hotels and shopping malls, or hailed from the street.

Bus: Dubai has an efficient modern bus service (tel: 800 9090, www.rta.ae); the main stations are the Gold Souk Bus Station in Deira and Al Ghubaiba in Bur Dubai (from where most services to other emirates depart). Unfortunately, local buses are aimed at low-income expats, and tend not to serve more upmarket tourist destinations. One exception is the handy bus #8, which runs from Al Ghubaiba all the way down the Jumeira Road to the Marina. For longer journeys, however, buses often offer a convenient means of transport – particularly for the traffic-plagued journey to Sharjah, as well as to Hatta, Al Ain and Abu Dhabi.

Abra: The best way to appreciate the Creek is to take a water taxi, or *abra* (see page 30). Fares are just Dhs1 for *abra* trips from Bur Dubai to Deira and vice versa. For Dhs100 you can charter your own for an hour.

Water bus: Air-conditioned water buses also serve various points on the Creek, costing Dhs4 per return journey (no single fares available), payable only with a Nol card. They're much less enjoyable than the city's *abras*, and are double the price.

Car: For a city that didn't have a single stretch of tarmac when oil was discovered, Dubai has excellent roads. All the major car rental agencies have offices here including Avis (tel: 04 295 7121), Budget (tel: 800 2722), Hertz (tel: 04 282 4422) and Thrifty (tel: 800 4770). Most driving licences will be sufficient; if in doubt, contact your agency in advance.

Remember to drive on the right, always carry your licence with you and never drink and drive – Dubai has a zero-tolerance policy on drink driving and the penalty for ignoring it is a potential jail term. Wearing seatbelts is compulsory for drivers and front-seat passengers, and children under 10 must not sit in the front passenger seat.

Speed limits are normally between 60kph (37mph) and 120kph (74mph). Lane discipline is bad, and reckless driving fairly common, so drive with caution at all times. On road signs, distances are indicated in kilometres.

If you're involved in a road accident, stop and wait for the police. A police report on every level of accident is required for insurance claims.

Visas and passports

Visas are available on arrival at Dubai International Airport for business and

Metro train on the Red Line

leisure travellers from 46 countries, including the UK, Ireland, most Western European countries, the US, Canada, Australia, and New Zealand. The visa (issued free on arrival) is valid for 30 days and can be renewed for a further 30 days at the Department of Immigration and Naturalisation (tel: 04 398 1010), near Trade Centre Roundabout, for Dhs625, although a visa run (flying or driving in and out of the country to get a new visa), will be cheaper.

Those who don't qualify for a visa on arrival, including South African citizens, can get a 30-day, non-renewable tourist visa through a hotel or tour operator sponsor. This should be arranged before entry to the UAE: visitors should ensure they have a copy of the visa with them and they should stop to collect the original at a designated desk in the airport before they head for passport control. The total cost is Dhs120.

W

Websites

The following websites are useful sources of information:

7Days www.7days.ae
AMEInfo www.ameinfo.com
Dubai Duty Free www.dubaidutyfree.com
Dubai International Airport www.dubaiairports.com
Dubai Municipality www.dm.gov.ae
Dubai Roads and Transport Authority **(RTA)** www.rta.ae
Emirates Airline www.emirates.com
Emirates Today www.emiratestodayonline.com
Government of Dubai Department of Tourism and Commerce Marketing www.visitdubai.com
Gulf News www.gulfnews.com
The National www.thenational.ae
UAE Ministry of Information and Culture www.uaeinteract.com
TimeOut Dubai www.timeoutdubai.com
ShortList www.shortlistdubai.com

Weights and measures

The metric system is used in Dubai.

What's on

For listings of events and happenings in Dubai up to 14 days in advance try www.timeoutdubai.com or http://whatson.ae. For planning further ahead, try www.dubai-online.com/events or www.whatsonwhen.com.

Women

Dubai is one of the easiest and safest places in the Middle East for lone women to travel around, and many feel comfortable on their own in the evening. In terms of personal security, women are generally safe, although it's wise to exercise standard precautions and do not accept lifts from men met in bars and nightclubs. Away from beaches and swimming pools, women are expected to dress modestly, as are men.

Arabic characters on the Grand Mosque's facade

LANGUAGE

Arabic is the official language of the UAE, though in Dubai and Abu Dhabi you may be lucky to hear it. With just 17 percent of the population comprising native Emiratis, English is the lingua franca, but you're more likely to hear Jindi, Urdu, Malayalam or even Tagalog spoken.

Nevertheless, learning a few words of Arabic is worth the effort if only to practise with the Egyptian hotel staff or Lebanese waiters. Any efforts in Arabic by foreigners – particularly Westerners – is hugely appreciated. If you can muster only one phrase, make it the classic Muslim greeting, *as-salaam alaykum*, which for many Arabs shows not just willing but respect towards their religion and culture.

Conversing with people

Hello (informal) *Marhaba*
Greetings (Lit: Peace be upon you; formal) *As-salaam alaykum*
Greetings to you too (response) *Wa alaykum asalaam*
Pleased to meet you/nice to have met you *Fursa sa'ida*
Goodbye *Ma'as/salama*
Thank you (very much) *Shukran (jazee-lan)*
You're welcome *Afwan*
Please *Min fadlak*
Yes *Na'am*

No *La*
How are you? (to a man) *Kef halak?*
How are you? (to a woman) *Kef halik*
My name is… *Ismi…*
I am… *Ana…*
Where are you (m/f) from? *Min wayn inta/inti?*
I am from… *Ana min…*
I'm here on vacation/holiday/business *ana fee ejaaza/fee rihlat 'aamal*
I'm going to… *ana dhaahib m/dhaa-hiba f ila…*
I'm staying at the…Hotel *ana naazil m/ naazila f fee funduq…*

Directions

How do I get to…? *Keef boosal lil…?*
Can you show me the way to…? *Mum-kin tdallini ala tareeq lil…?*
How many kilometres? *Kam kilometr?*
To/for *Lil*
Left *Shimaal/yasaar*
Right *Yimeen*
Straight *Sida*
Number *Raqam*
City *Madina*
There *Hina/hinak*
This way *Matn hina*
In front of *Qiddaam*
Near *Gareeb*
Far *Ba'aed*
North *Shimaal*
South *Janub*
East *Sharq*
West *Gharb*

Street signs and directions in Dubai

Eating out

Restaurant *Al mataam*
May I have the menu? *Ana areed al-kaart?*
Do you have...? *Haal indaak...?*
Does anyone here speak English? *Haal yoogaad ahad yatakaallam ingleezi?*
What do you recommend? *Bi madha tinsahnee?*
Do you have vegetarian dishes? *Haal indaak akl nabati laahm?*
I don't eat meat *Ana ma bakul laham*
I am a vegetarian *Ána nabbáti (for a man)/nabbátiya (for a woman)*
Nothing more, thanks *Kafee mash-kur*
Just a small portion *Miqdaar sager*
I'd like the bill, please *Ana areed al-hisaab min fadlak*
Delicious! *Ladheedh!*
That was delicious *Kan al aakl ladheedh*
Toilet *Al hammam*

Food and drink

restaurant *máta'am*
breakfast *futour*
lunch *ghadaa*
dinner *ashaa*
food *ákl*
fish *simich*
meat *láhm*
chicken *dijaj*
mutton *ghanam*
milk *halíb*
cheese *jabne*
butter *zibdeh*

eggs *bayd*
bread *khúbz*
salad *saláta*
honey *'asl*
yoghurt *laban*
jam *murabbeh*
dates *balah*
olives *zatoon*
delicious *ladhidh*
coffee *káhwa*
tea *shay*
beer *beera*
cup *finján*
with sugar *bi súkkar*
without sugar *bidún súkkar*
mineral water *mái ma'adaniya*
glass *gelaas*
bottle *zajaja/botel*

Emergencies

Help me! *Saa' idoonee!*
I'm ill! *Ana mareed/mareeda (m/f)!*
Call the police! *Itasell bil shurta!*
The doctor *Al tabeeb*
Hospital *Al mustashfa*
Police *Al shurta*
Go away/get lost! *Seer!*
Shame on you (if harassed)! *istiHi a'la Haalak!*

Health

I'm unwell *Ana maareed*
My friend is unwell *Sadeeyee maareed*
I'm allergic... *Andee hasasiyya...*
to antibiotics *min al mudad alhayawee*
to aspirin *min al asbireen*

Abu Dhabi taxi

to nuts *min al mukassarat*
to penicillin *min al binisileen*
I want... *Ana areed...*
Antiseptic *Mutahhir*
Chemist/pharmacy *Al sayidaliyya*
Condoms *Kaboot*
I am/I have... *Ana...*
Diarrhoea *Is-haal*
Fever *Sukhooma*
Headache *Suda' ras/waja' ras*
Pregnant *Haamel*
Prescription *Wasfa/rashetta*
Stomach ache *Waja' feel bat-n*
Sun-block cream *Marham wagee min ashat al shams*
Sanitary towels/tampons *Fuwat saHi-yya leel Hareem*

Language difficulties

Do you speak English/French/German *Tatkallam ingleezi/fransawi/almaani?*
I understand (by a man) *Ana fahim*
I understand (by a woman) *Ana fahma*
I don't understand (by a man) *Ana ma fahim*
I don't understand (by a woman) *Ana ma fahma*
I don't speak Arabic *Ma atkallam arabi*
Could you write it down, please? *Mumkin tiktbha lee, min fadlak?*
Speak more slowly *Takalam shwai shwai*

Services

The bank *Al bank*
Post office *Maktab al bareed*

Telephone *Al telefon/al hataf*
I want to change... *Ana abga asrif...*
Money *Floos*
Travellers' cheques *Sheikat seeya-Heeya*
Embassy *As safara*

Shopping

Where can I buy...?' *Wein agdar ashtiri...?*
Do you have...(to a man)? *Indik?*
Do you have... (to a woman)? *Indich?*
What is this? *Shoo Hadha?*
How much? *Bikam?*
How many? *Kam?*
It's too expensive *Ghalee/ghalia wa'id (m/f)*
There isn't (any) *Mafee (walashai)*
Can I look at it? *Mumkin ashoof il?*
What time does it open? *Sa'a kam yeftaH?*
What time does it close? *Sa'a kam yebannad?*

Sightseeing

Where is the...? *Wein al...?*
Beach *Il shaat'i*
Souk *Al souq*
Mosque *Al masjid*
Museum *Al matHaf*
The Old City *Al madina al qadima*
Tourism office *Maktab al seeyaHa*

Useful phrases

Good/OK *Kweis/tayib/zein*
No problem *Mafee mushkala/Mafi mushkil*
Impossible *Mish mumkin*

Ruling Family poster

Magazines for sale

It doesn't matter/I don't mind *Ma'alish*
God willing (when talking about any future event or wish) *Insha'allah*
I like (Dubai) *Ana bHib (dubay)*
I don't like... *Ana ma bHib*
Excuse me (to a man) *Lau samaHt*
Excuse me (to a woman) *Lau samaHti*
After you *Atfaddal*

Social media

Are you on Facebook/Twitter? *Hal ladayk hisaab 'ala feesbook/tweetir*
What's your username? *Ma ism al-mustakhdim al-khaas beek*
I'll add you as a friend *Sa-a deefak ka-sadeeq*
I'll follow you on Twitter *Sa-ataabi'ka 'ala tweetir*
Are you following...? *Hal tutaabi'...?*
I'll put the pictures on Facebook/Twitter *Sa-udi' as-suwwar 'ala feesbook/tweetir*
I'll tag you in the pictures *Sa-udi' ismak 'ala as-suwwar*

Days and numbers

today *al yoom*
tomorrow *bokhra*
yesterday *ams*
early *mbach'ir/badri*
late *mit'akhir*
day *yoom*
night *layl*
Monday *yoom al ithnayn*
Tuesday *yoom ath thalatha*
Wednesday *yoom al araba'a*
Thursday *yoom al khamees*
Friday *yoom al jum'a*
Saturday *yoom as sabt*
Sunday *yoom al had*
zero *sifir*
one *wáhid*
two *ithnayn*
three *taláta*
four *árba'a*
five *khámsa*
six *sítta*
seven *sába'a*
eight *tamánia*
nine *tísa'a*
ten *áshara*
eleven *hidáshar*
twelve *itnáshar*
twenty *áishreen*
twenty-one *wáhid wa áishreen*
twenty-two *ithnayn wa áishreen*
thirty *thalatheen*
forty *arba'een*
fifty *khamseen*
sixty *sitteen*
seventy *saba'een*
eighty *thimaneen*
ninety *tis'een*
one hundred *maya*
one hundred and fifty *may wa khamseen*
two hundred *mayatayn*
three hundred *thaltamaya*
four hundred *rab'amaya*
five hundred *khamsamaya*
six hundred *sittamaya*
seven hundred *sabamaya*
eight hundred *tamnamaya*
nine hundred *tissamaya*
one thousand *alf*

Syriana was filmed in the UAE

BOOKS AND FILM

Dubai doesn't have quite the range of books written about it – especially in the English language – or fiction based in it, as elsewhere in the world. Books tend to be either about the city or country's 'ancient' history (pre- and post-formation of the United Arab Emirates in 1971); the rise of the modern cities and nation we know today, with its incredible ambition and dramatic rate of growth and advancement; while in recent years, fiction based in modern Dubai has begun to emerge. Some of the best reads are the tales of the people who saw the country grow in just a few short decades from a collection of tribes living in fishing villages to the staggering modern metropolises which are now players on the world stage.

Books

Beyond Dubai: Seeking Lost Cities in the Emirates, David Millar. An enjoyable travelogue exploring the Emirates and its history.

Dubai Dreams: Inside the Kingdom of Bling, Raymond Barrett. Intermittently entertaining portrait of the 21st-century city, mixing travelogue, history and reportage.

Dubai: Gilded Cage, Syed Ali Dubai. Perceptive look at the role and status of Dubai's massive expat community, from Indian labourers to wealthy Western execs.

Dubai: the Story of the World's Fastest City (published in North America as ***City of Gold: Dubai and the Dream of Capitalism***), Jim Krane. Superbly readable and perceptive portrait of the modern city. Essential reading for anyone interested in the 21st-century Gulf and what makes the modern metropolis tick.

Dubai: the Vulnerability of Success, Christopher M. Davidson. Detailed scholarly history of Dubai, accompanied by chapters on the city's social, political and economic workings.

Rashid's Legacy: the Genesis of the Maktoum Family, Graeme Wilson. Depicts the family's history and approach to transforming Dubai.

Sheikh Zayed Life and Times 1918–2004, through the lens of Noor Ali Rashid. The history of a nation personified in its founder.

Telling Tales: an Oral History of Dubai, Julia Wheeler. Photographs accompany insights from some of Dubai's founding citizens. Written by a BBC Gulf correspondent.

Mother without a Mask, Patricia Holton. A rare, insightful story from a Westerner who manage to explore Arabic culture from her access inside an Emirati family.

This Strange Eventful History: Memoirs of Earlier Days in the UAE and Oman, Edward Henderson. A good account of how the country evolved.

Tom Cruise climbs the Burj Khalifa in Mission Impossible – Ghost Protocol

Arabia (Through the Looking Glass), Jonathan Raban. An excellent and amusing overview of the different Gulf and Middle Eastern countries, offering a fascinating record of the region during a period of immense change.

Arabian Destiny, Edward Henderson. Fascinating autobiography covering Henderson's time in Dubai in the late 1940s and early 1950s and his a gripping account of the country's evolution as well as delicate negotiations with the Omani tribes during the exploration for oil.

Arabian Sands, Wilfred Thesiger. Journeys made from 1945–50 in and around the Empty Quarter of Oman, Saudi Arabia and the UAE.

Dubai, Robin Moore. Blockbuster novel by **French Connection** author Robin Moore, set in late 1960s Dubai and with a Hollywood-style cast of arms dealers, gold smugglers, oil-prospectors and other soldiers of fortune.

Dubai Tales, Mohammed al Murr. Short stories set in Dubai and area.

Dubai Wives, Zvezdana Rashkovich. An entertaining novel set in Dubai from an author who is a Dubai wife herself.

The Sand Fish: a Novel from Dubai, Maha Gargash. Dubai and the northern UAE during the 1950s seen through the eyes of a rebellious teenage girl.

Sandstorms – Days and Nights in Arabia, Peter Theroux. Amusing observations of expatriate life.

The Son of a Duck is a Floater, Primrose Arnander and Ashkhain Skipwith. A collection of Arab proverbs and sayings.

Travels with a Tangerine: a Journey in the Footnotes of Ibn Battutah, Tim Mackintosh-Smith. Beautifully observed account of Mackintosh-Smith's journey through the Middle East following in the footsteps of Ibn Battuta, with two fine chapters on Oman.

The Wink of the Mona Lisa, Mohammed al Murr. Short stories by a leading UAE writer.

Dubai: A City Portrait, Patrick Lichfield. Lavish coffee-table book.

Dubai 24 Hours, by Michael Tobias. The city as experienced by a team of Dubai's leading photographers during the course of a single day.

Dubai: the Arabian Dream, David Saunders. Account of Dubai's rapid development, illustrated with many stunning photographs.

The Emirates by the First Photographers, William Facey and Gillian Grant. Historical photographs of the region.

The UAE Formative Years, 1965–75. A Collection of Historical Photographs, Ramesh Shukla.

The UAE: Visions of Change, Noor Ali Rashid. Photographs from 1958 to 1997.

Film

While Arabic and Emirati culture, including filmmaking, receive a lot of support, there have been no classic films made in the UAE in the English language and appearances in international films are limited to palace (hotel resort) shots for blockbusters like *Syriana*, or The Empty Quarter desert for *Star Wars*.

ABOUT THIS BOOK

This *Explore Guide* has been produced by the editors of Insight Guides, whose books have set the standard for visual travel guides since 1970. With top-quality photography and authoritative recommendations, these guidebooks bring you the very best routes and itineraries in the world's most exciting destinations.

BEST ROUTES

The routes in the book provide something to suit all budgets, tastes and trip lengths. As well as covering the destination's many classic attractions, the itineraries track lesser-known sights, and there are also excursions for those who want to extend their visit outside the city. The routes embrace a range of interests, so whether you are an art fan, a gourmet, a history buff or have kids to entertain, you will find an option to suit.

We recommend reading the whole of a route before setting out. This should help you to familiarise yourself with it and enable you to plan where to stop for refreshments – options are shown in the 'Food and Drink' box at the end of each tour.

For our pick of the tours by theme, consult Recommended Routes for… (see pages 6–7).

INTRODUCTION

The routes are set in context by this introductory section, giving an overview of the destination to set the scene, plus background information on food and drink, shopping and more, while a succinct history timeline highlights the key events over the centuries.

DIRECTORY

Also supporting the routes is a Directory chapter, with a clearly organised A–Z of practical information, our pick of where to stay while you are there and select restaurant listings; these eateries complement the more low-key cafés and restaurants that feature within the routes and are intended to offer a wider choice for evening dining. Also included here are some nightlife listings, plus a handy language guide and our recommendations for books and films about the destination.

ABOUT THE AUTHORS

This new guide to Dubai was written by UK-based travel writer and editor Tim Binks. Tim lived in Dubai for eight years in two separate stints between 1996 and 2009 – bridging the leap Dubai made to be a major city on the world stage, and witnessing its phenomenal growth – as well as revisiting the country several times since. In addition to exploring the UAE and neighbouring Oman, and writing for guidebooks on these destinations, he has also worked on travel guides for other places in the Middle East, Europe and Asia, including other books for Insight Guides as an editor. This edition builds on the previous work of Gavin Thomas and Matt Jones.

CONTACT THE EDITORS

We hope you find this Explore Guide useful, interesting and a pleasure to read. If you have any questions or feedback on the text, pictures or maps, please do let us know. If you have noticed any errors or outdated facts, or have suggestions for places to include on the routes, we would be delighted to hear from you. Please drop us an email at hello@insightguides.com. Thanks!

CREDITS

Explore Dubai
Editor: Sarah Clark
Author: Tim Binks
Head of Production: Rebeka Davies
Picture Editor: Tom Smyth
Cartography: original cartography B&B Dubai, updated by Carte
Photo credits: Alamy 71L, 136, 137; Atlantis, The Palm 26ML, 26MR, 64; Chris Bradley/Apa Publications 12/13, 83, 84, 85L, 84/85, 92, 93L, 92/93, 129, 130, 134, 134/135; FRHI Hotels & Resorts 45L, 104; Getty Images 1, 4/5T, 6TL, 6BC, 7MR, 8ML, 8MR, 8/9T, 10, 11, 12, 14/15, 18/19, 20, 21L, 20/21, 22, 23, 24, 25, 26/27T, 32, 33, 37, 39L, 43, 44/45, 48/49, 53, 56, 57, 58, 61, 62, 62/63, 66/67, 70/71, 74, 75, 76, 77L, 76/77, 80, 86, 87, 90, 94, 95, 97, 100/101T, 114, 116, 119, 123, 125, 126, 127, 128; Hilton Hotels & Resorts 102, 109; Hyatt Corperation 4MR, 103, 108, 111; iStock 4ML, 4MR, 4MC, 6MC, 6ML, 7T, 7MR, 17L, 18, 26MC, 30, 38, 40, 44, 46, 47, 51L, 55, 63L, 66, 68/69, 72, 88, 89L, 88/89, 91, 99L, 122, 131; Jumeirah International 4MC, 4ML, 8MC, 8MC, 8MR, 13L, 16, 16/17, 50, 59L, 58/59, 60, 100ML, 100MC, 100MR, 100MR, 100MC, 100ML, 106, 110, 112, 113, 115, 117, 124; Kevin Cummins/Apa Publications 26MR, 78, 82, 98/99, 135L; One&Only 65, 107; Paul Thuysbaert Photography/Arabian Adventure 70; Shangri-La International 105; Shutterstock 7M, 8ML, 19L, 26MC, 26ML, 28, 29L, 28/29, 31, 34, 35, 36, 38/39, 41, 42, 50/51, 52, 67L, 73, 79, 81L, 80/81, 96, 98, 118, 120/121, 132, 133; The Address Hotels + Resorts 54
Cover credits: iStock (main) Shutterstock (bottom)

Printed by CTPS – China

All Rights Reserved
© 2017 Apa Digital (CH) AG and Apa Publications (UK) Ltd

First Edition 2017

DISTRIBUTION

UK, Ireland and Europe
Apa Publications (UK) Ltd
sales@insightguides.com
United States and Canada
Ingram Publisher Services
ips@ingramcontent.com
Australia and New Zealand
Woodslane
info@woodslane.com.au
Southeast Asia
Apa Publications (Singapore) Pte
singaporeoffice@insightguides.com
Hong Kong, Taiwan and China
Apa Publications (HK) Ltd
hongkongoffice@insightguides.com
Worldwide
Apa Publications (UK) Ltd
sales@insightguides.com

SPECIAL SALES, CONTENT LICENSING AND COPUBLISHING

Insight Guides can be purchased in bulk quantities at discounted prices. We can create special editions, personalised jackets and corporate imprints tailored to your needs.
sales@insightguides.com
www.insightguides.biz

3 1907 00378 6620

INDEX